JB JOSSEY-BASS™
A Wiley Brand

T0319408

Naming Gift Opportunities

How to Successfully Secure More Naming Gifts

Scott C. Stevenson, Editor

WILEY

NAMING GIFT OPPORTUNITIES:

How to Successfully Secure More Naming Gifts

Published by

Stevenson, Inc.

P.O. Box 4528 • Sioux City, Iowa • 51104

Phone 712.239.3010 • Fax 712.239.2166

www.stevensoninc.com

TABLE OF CONTENTS

TABLE OF CONTENTS

NAMING GIFT OPPORTUNITIES: How to Successfully Secure More Naming Gifts

NAMING GIFT POLICIES

Any nonprofit actively engaged in encouraging, accepting and publicizing named gifts should have a policy in place that addresses naming gift procedures and questions that may arise. Such a policy benefits both the donor and the nonprofit and should be regularly reviewed and approved by your board of trustees.

Create a Policy for Accepting Corporate, Naming Gifts

When a nonprofit accepts a major naming gift or enters into a marketing co-venture with a company, the name of the nonprofit becomes linked with its partners, and any negative press and impressions of that company will affect the nonprofit, says Theresa Nelson, principal, Theresa Nelson & Associates (Oakland, CA).

Nonprofits should enter into such a partnership only after a rigorous, objective process to create a gift acceptance policy outlining the criteria that must first be met, Nelson says. That criteria should include whether the company is a good fit with the nonprofit's mission; what would be required of your organization; and a risk analysis.

Take into consideration negative outcomes of a corporate gift before accepting.

"You need to ask yourselves, 'Will this corporate naming opportunity put us at high risk for negative publicity?'" she says. "Above all, you need to protect your own interests. You need to have an escape clause in case the company brings bad publicity to your organization. When something hurts the identity of your organization, it turns away donors and affects your reputation and ability to raise funds."

Address the issue of major corporate naming before it becomes a reality, says Nelson, because once you have one group excited about a gift, and one group opposed, the question changes from whether you will accept naming gifts from companies at all, to "do we like this company," which can become a very heated issue.

Other areas to address in a corporate gift acceptance policy, she says, include:

- Any exceptions, e.g. corporations that you would never take donations from under any circumstances.

- Levels of recognition.

- What permanent naming privileges to offer, or if you should even offer naming opportunities to corporations.

"Organizations can normally easily determine companies they would always take gifts from and those they would never take gifts from," says Nelson, "but it's the ones in the middle that require some thought — and a gift acceptance policy."

Source: Theresa Nelson, Principal, Theresa Nelson & Associates, Oakland, CA. Phone (510) 420-0539.
E-mail: nelsontm@pacbell.net

Naming Policy Considerations

Here are some of the considerations that your naming gifts policy should address:

- ✓ Size of a gift required to name a physical space or endowed fund.

- ✓ Requirement of establishing an endowment to support the overhead and maintenance of the named facility.

- ✓ Availability of naming existing spaces that have never been named.

- ✓ How to address already named spaces and facilities that will be demolished or renovated.

- ✓ Whether the naming of a building or an area requires a completed gift agreement and receipt of cash or assets that can be converted to cash immediately.

- ✓ Whether buildings will be named in honor of a donor in return for an estate commitment.

- ✓ The design, wording and placement of plaques that recognize donors.

- ✓ The appropriateness of naming spaces, facilities, endowments or programs based on extraordinary service rather than a particular gift amount.

NAMING GIFT POLICIES

Develop Your Unique Plan of Naming Gift Opportunities

When evaluating your organization's unique naming gift opportunities it helps to have a worksheet and some procedures to follow. Identified below are some key procedures:

A. Assemble a group of key staff — and key board members, volunteers and donors, if appropriate. Conduct a brainstorming session to identify all naming possibilities, pointing out that any ideas are worth considering. Come up with as many suggestions as possible.

B. Meet again, this time using key staff only, to review the list of naming possibilities. Prioritize the list based on a) need for support, b) donor attractiveness and c) dollar amount potential.

C. Use your prioritized list of ideas to craft a printed menu of naming gift opportunities that can be included in various marketing literature as you prepare to share these opportunities with select prospects.

A worksheet will help staff organize and identify all naming opportunities.

NAMING GIFT OPPORTUNITIES WORKSHEET

Date _____ Submitted By _____

Identified Naming Gift Opportunity (building, space, endowed fund)
_____
_____

Estimated Gift Range Required to Name This Project/Facility/Fund:
$ _____ to $ _____

Gift to be used to cover the cost of:
_____
_____

Prospects who may be interested in naming this project/facility/fund:
1. _____

Possible names to consider for the project/facility/fund:
a) _____
b) _____
c) _____

2. _____

Possible names to consider for the project/facility/fund:
a) _____
b) _____
c) _____

3. _____

Possible names to consider for the project/facility/fund:
a) _____
b) _____
c) _____

Return this completed form to Office of Institutional Advancement

NAMING GIFT POLICIES

Handling Former Named Spaces When Renovating a Facility

A donor's major gift is enabling you to renovate an existing named building. The name of the new donor will replace that of the former named donor. Plans include renovation of interior spaces, and you want to solicit donors to rename those spaces. Should you continue to honor former donors — especially the former named donor? If so, how?

Here, three fundraising experts share their thoughts:

Karen Logan, stewardship officer for Queen's University in Kingston, Ontario, suggests contacting the families to let them know that you are committed to keeping the names alive in the facility, even if it is not in the same format. "Try to involve the family of the earlier donors as much as possible so that no one is caught off guard," she says. "You might want to consider putting all of the former named spaces on one plaque and give it a place of importance."

When creating a naming policy, says Logan, it's best to not make any commitment to keep a named space once a facility has been torn down or renovated.

Lisa C. Honan, senior director of donor relations, Syracuse (NY) University, says that when building a new facility for an existing school or organization, name part of the new facility for the prior building's donors. "Or, you could put a plaque up in a reasonably (but not too) prominent location that indicates your organization's gratitude for the prior donor's support. We're doing that with all room names for our prior School of Management building. The donors are not naming new rooms in the new building, but we're recognizing them on a plaque as longtime supporters of the school."

Patricia Kight, associate director of donor relations and recognition for the University of Minnesota Foundation, suggests pulling together several reasonable scenarios for recognizing the former named donor, and then having your organization's president or board chair sit down with the former donor and see which scenario he or she prefers. "Perhaps that donor could somehow be involved in the dedication of the new facility — in a lesser role than the new named donor of course — but honored as someone who has provided major support to your organization in the past."

Sources: Karen Logan, Stewardship Officer, Queen's University, Summerhill, Kingston ON. Phone (613) 533-2060 ext. 74122. E-mail: Logank@post.queensu.can

Lisa C. Honan, Senior Director, Donor Relations, Syracuse University, Syracuse, NY. Phone (315) 443-3580. E-mail: lchonan@syr.edu

Patricia Kight, Associate Director, Donor Relations and Recognition, University of Minnesota Foundation, Minneapolis, MN 55455. Phone (612) 626-8139. E-mail: kight001@umn.edu

Have a plan that recognizes all donors — past and present — when renovating facilities.

Wording Tips for Your Naming Gift Policy

Do you have a naming gift policy in place? Christine Clouse, director of university relations for Midwestern University (Glendale, AZ), shares these two points for drafting a named gifts policy:

1. If the gift relates to a facility, include that the naming opportunity is for the useful life of the building. "That way, if the building needs to be torn down at some point in the future, you aren't in a quandary," she says.

2. Use the terminology "commemorative" opportunity rather than the word "naming." "I believe it speaks to the heart of the matter better and bodes well with prospective donors," she says.

Sources: Christine Clouse, Director of University Relations, Midwestern University, Glendale, AZ. Phone (623) 572-3286. E-mail: cclous@midwestern.edu

NAMING GIFT POLICIES

Carry on Name When Building Is No More

 We are demolishing a named building. What are some ways we can continue to honor the donor?

"In the recent past, we have had several buildings which were remodeled extensively. In all of those cases, we paid tribute to the original name through appropriate displays in the entrance foyer of the newly renovated buildings."

— Denise H. Howard, Director of Donor Relations, Davidson College, Davidson, NC. Phone (704) 894-2102. E-mail: dehoward@davidson.edu

"We are demolishing our library this spring. We have named a collection of books in the new library for the soon-to-be-demolished building. We also have that family's name on the donor wall in the new library. We included the family in the dedication ceremony of the new building."

— Andi Jones, Associate Director of Stewardship, Valparaiso University, Valparaiso, IN. Phone (219) 464-5321. E-mail: andi.jones@valpo.edu

If you are demolishing or remodeling something with a named gift associated with it, honor previous donors by involving them in the dedication.

Be Prepared for Naming Gift Consequences

"We are drafting a naming opportunity policy. We would like to include a guideline that would allow us to withdraw the naming if the donor were to do something that would bring negative attention to our organization. How should such a guideline be worded, what are the benefits of having one, and have you ever had to enforce it?"

Southern Alberta Institute of Technology (SAIT) included the following guideline in its naming opportunity policy/procedure allowing them to withdraw a naming opportunity under certain circumstances: *When a person, organization, foundation or corporation's activities reflect negatively on SAIT's public image, or are in material conflict with SAIT's mission and/or policies, then SAIT has the right to terminate the naming even if such naming was originally deemed to be in perpetuity.*

"When issues around ENRON and WorldCom and others became public, it reinforced a belief that we would need to be able to respond to protect our own brand and reputation if an existing naming should come under fire," says Cindy Neufeld, stewardship coordinator.

She also created a letter of understanding that outlines what the naming is for, the board-approved name and the length of the naming. "Donors read and sign this letter, so there is no lack of awareness should there ever be a reason to withdraw it," she says.

Since SAIT's naming policy is relatively new — less than five years, says Neufeld, they've never had to enforce it.

Source: Cindy Neufeld, CFRE, Stewardship Coordinator, Southern Alberta Institute of Technology (SAIT), Calgary, Alberta. Phone (403) 284-8925. E-mail: cindy.neufeld@sait.ca Website: www.sait.ca/alumniandfriends

Know That Named Structures Should Remain Permanent

Your organization's recently completed strategic plan calls for tearing down a portion of a building to make way for significant improvements. But some of what is to be removed includes named rooms: a dining room, a lounge, offices and more.

What becomes of those spaces that were named in honor of the donors? Are they to be forgotten after the bulldozer does its job? No way.

If your renovation plans call for eliminating named spaces (or even buildings), it's important to somehow reincorporate those names into your new or updated facility. Work with the families or businesses that provided the naming gifts. Together, come up with an alternative that meets with both sides' approval.

If you take the proper steps to carry on acknowledgment, you may even convince each party involved to make a new gift that would endow the renovated space to continue to bear the name of the original donor.

NAMING GIFT POLICIES

Naming Opportunities in Perpetuity — Good or Bad Idea?

Many organizations specify that their naming opportunities are in perpetuity, but is that really a good idea? Perpetual commitments can cause interesting problems, says Tim Mills-Groninger, associate executive director of IT Resource Center in Chicago. "Best practice indicates that any agreements include the conditions that will cancel or otherwise redirect the endowment," he says. Examples of those conditions include:

- The donor or the donor's family engages in types of public activities that put the named entity into a bad light.

- The principal no longer generates income sufficient to support the project.

- The original purpose of intent of the fund is no longer relevant.

Purdue University considers the naming of a facility a permanent act, but in its policy, Naming of New and Renovated University Facilities, it includes wording that gives it an out ("...and it is expected that the designated name will not change except under extraordinary circumstances.").

"I do not know of any situation in which we have changed a naming and we look at this as a permanent act, but if something extraordinary happens we reserve the right to act to protect the university," says Caroline Gery, assistant director for development.

Sources: Tim Mills-Groninger, Associate Executive Director, IT Resource Center, Chicago, IL. Phone (312) 372-4872 ext. 132. E-mail: timmg@itresourcecenter.org
Caroline Gery, Assistant Director of Development, Purdue University, West Lafayette, IN. Phone (765) 494-6902. E-mail: cgery@purdue.edu

Naming gift policies should take extraordinary circumstances into consideration.

Explore the Notion of a Naming Something Temporarily

No one willing to step forward with the size of gift it would take to permanently name an office, room or wing of your facility? Until the right person emerges, consider the idea of naming something for a year at a time.

Let's say you have an attractive seminar room at your facility that, if permanently endowed and named, would go for $100,000. Annual endowment income of 7 percent would make $7,000 in maintenance and enhancement funds available for the room each year. But, since no one has yet stepped forward to permanently endow the room, perhaps you could find a business or individual willing to contribute, say $5,000, to have his/her name on the room for a one-year period.

The concept is worth exploring. Although naming gifts of a finite period are rare, a limited time naming gift would produce multiple benefits:

- The donor gets the benefit of having his/her name on that particular room or wing or office for a year's time.

- The donor is given the opportunity to see his/her gift used for a specific purpose (e.g., purchasing new equipment for a room, covering the room's maintenance costs, having an office or room redecorated or any number of specific possibilities).

- The yearlong named room might help others become interested in permanently naming that particular project.

- The charity is able to generate a gift that might not otherwise have come about.

Explore the concept of yearlong naming gifts. Discuss it as a staff. Bring it up to your board's development committee. Test it out with a handful of businesses or individuals. You just might have a new method for generating sizeable gifts and adding another motivational strategy that encourages larger, permanently endowed gifts.

If no one is willing to step foward with a large gift to permantly name something, consider the idea of a temporary naming opportunity.

NAMING GIFT POLICIES

Should Naming Rights Have Limits?

Nonprofits are increasingly using naming opportunities to recognize major gifts. But namings can go awry. A donor could — after the organization has already etched his/her name on the building and printed new materials — become delinquent on pledge payments, ensnared in a public scandal or die before full payment is made.

So what's a nonprofit organization to do? Take situations on a case-by-case basis, says William Krueger, president, Capital Quest, Inc. (Louisville, TN).

Krueger says he doubts anyone could write a donor agreement that met all possible negative naming scenarios, and shouldn't try: "We're building relationships, not contractual agreements here. Like they should with every donor, nonprofits should develop individual strategies for problems that may come up and try to avoid creating policies that cover all options. We had a client once who received an offer of a $100,000 gift from Pepsi to put Pepsi's logo on the scoreboard. The client turned it down, saying it was worth $200,000 because that was how it was listed in the beginning of the campaign! That shows what happens when something is viewed as policy instead of guidance."

While some high-profile issues may arise regarding namings, the reality is that most naming efforts are excellent donor recognition tools, he says. "The trick is to remember they are donor recognition tools, not sales vehicles. Donors who only give to get a name on an building, wing or room, without buying into the mission and vision of the organization, are the ones who create the most problems later."

For a donor just seeking to get his/her name on a building, Krueger says it's a contest with a cost-versus-value mentality: "Especially when that donor is pledging as opposed to giving cash, the conflict is created when the donor feels they've already received all the value, but still have to pay for the gift they made three or four years ago. Then the value is zero, in the donor's mind, but the cost is great."

When a naming goes bad, Krueger says, it's not the crime, but the cover-up that can get you in trouble: "Be open and honest about what happened, never trying to show up the donor, and move along. There really are worse things than a building named after someone who didn't fulfill their gift."

Source: William Krueger, President, Capital Quest, Inc., Louisville, TN. Phone (800) 263-1976. E-mail: bill@capitalcampaigns.com

When it comes to naming rights, most agree they should be considered on a case-by-case basis.

Organization Offers 10-Year, 20-Year Naming Opportunities

Officials with The Pittsburgh Symphony Orchestra (PSO) of Pittsburgh, PA, recently launched an $80 million Commitment to Excellence campaign to substantially enlarge its endowment.

"To recognize and thank those donors who make significant gifts to the campaign, the PSO is offering donors the opportunity to endow musicians' chairs, educational programs, and public and administrative spaces with terms of 10 years, 20 years and in perpetuity," says Jodi Weisfield, associate director of the major campaign.

The financial requirements begin with a donation of $25,000 to $2.5 million.

"PSO's naming opportunities are available at many price points, so that donors who wish to contribute have the option to do so at a cost that is comfortable for them and can choose the opportunity that is most meaningful," Weisfield says.

When the term expires, donors have the option of renewing. If they choose not to, the naming opportunity will be available to other donors.

"Through this recognition, we're able to showcase the generosity and commitment of the donors who make it possible to have a world-class symphony in Pittsburgh. This campaign gives us the chance to bring it to people's attention as a way to support the orchestra."

Source: Jodi Weisfield, Associate Director of the Major Campaign, The Pittsburgh Symphony Orchestra, Pittsburgh, PA.

NAMING GIFT OPPORTUNITIES: How to Successfully Secure More Naming Gifts

IDENTIFYING NAMING OPPORTUNITIES

There are no limits when it comes to naming opportunities that might be available and appropriate. Study your nonprofit's budget and existing programs to discover what might be funded with a naming gift. Walk around your campus or facilities and take notes. Pay attention to the naming gifts that are being established at all types of charities to develop your own menu of naming opportunities.

Dream of What Could Be

Naming gift possibilities are only limited by your imagination.

It doesn't matter whether you represent a college, university, youth organization, social service agency, symphony, medical center or other worthy cause — naming gift opportunities are only limited by your imagination. What one donor may consider an outlandish naming opportunity, another may find to be right on target.

That's why it's in your best interest to identify as many legitimate naming opportunities as possible for your organization. Brainstorm the possibilities with staff, board members, key volunteers and donors. Dream of what could be.

Once you have identified as many naming gift opportunities as possible, you can begin the process of prioritizing them internally, measuring which gift opportunities are more needed and more practical based on your organization's mission, services and strategic plans for the future.

Regardless of what you decide to market as gift opportunities down the road, you will find it immensely helpful to have a menu of naming opportunities at hand as you meet with and cultivate potential donors.

Don't Overlook Naming Unconventional Spaces

While many organizations are now offering naming opportunities for buildings and rooms within buildings, others are beginning to offer the opportunity to name more unconventional spaces such as a student information desk, a hallway, or even a view. How do you go about assessing the value of naming such a space?

An unwritten rule used by Eastern Illinois University's Office of Development when valuing unconventional spaces is: How much public exposure will the area have, or how large or important is the space? says Nancy C. Page, donor relations officer.

In the Neal Welcome Center, where Page's office is located, the foyer or entryway has considerable public exposure. "Everyone who enters the building passes through there," she says. "However, it is not a place where people linger. Therefore, it was $20,000 to name the entry way."

As you consider more unconventional spaces as naming possibilities, consider their degree of public exposure as well as the size of the space.

Offices where people spend more time, and which have more space than the entryway, are named for $25,000, says Page: "The conference room, which is the largest room in the building and where people spend more time, was named for $100,000."

Erin Warnke, assistant director of donor relations for Brandeis University, says they have no official guidelines for naming unconventional spaces; they are usually priced on a case-by-case basis. "Usually, the prices for these have previously been named in a menu of opportunities," she says. One thing you have to consider in naming these spaces, she says, is not only what the space is naming, but also what this prevents you from naming: "For example, if you hang a plaque up recognizing the space, and it's in the middle of a wing, will you still be able to sell the wing?"

Sources: Nancy C. Page, Donor Relations Officer, Office of Development, Eastern Illinois University, Charleston, IL. Phone (217) 581-3314. E-mail: ncpage@eiu.edu
Erin Warnke, Assistant Director of Donor Relations, Brandeis University, Waltham, MA. Phone (781) 736-4064. E-mail: warnke@brandeis.edu

IDENTIFYING NAMING OPPORTUNITIES

Keep an Open Mind When Considering Named Gift Options

Never overlook a potential naming idea, especially if initiated by the would-be donor.

The University of Colorado (Boulder, CO) received a $25,000 gift from venture capitalist Brad Feld to name a bathroom in its ATLAS Institute that opened in 2006.

The men's lavatory features a plaque with Feld's words of wisdom: "The best ideas often come at inconvenient times — don't ever close your mind to them."

Feld had made a similar proposal to his alma mater, MIT, which was rejected. University spokesman Bruce Henderson says more bathrooms are available to name.

Source: Bruce Henderson, ATLAS Administration, University of Colorado at Boulder, Boulder, CO. E-mail: Bruce.Henderson@Colorado.edu

Many Naming Opportunities Result in Many Gifts

Your list of naming gift opportunities should be ever changing.

Are you sure you have identified all of your charity's naming gift opportunities?

Donors have named thousands of items in the past years at Cottey College (Nevada, MO), says Wendy MacLaren, vice president of institutional advancement. These include everything from chairs and tables to buildings and outdoor areas.

While they're open to naming just about anything, they do have a few rules: The item has to be worth $500 or more (in both the cost of the item and the value of the recognition); and it cannot be a consumable item (such as a computer that will be replaced in a couple of years). Books are the only exception to this rule, and can be named for the book's cost.

"We like to do things that make our donors feel good and benefit the institution at the same time," says MacLaren. "Naming opportunities are what is important to our constituents. It's what motivates them to want to contribute. If the institution needs XYZ and we have donors who want to pay tribute to someone and XYZ fits the bill, why not put a small plaque on it?"

The college's list of naming opportunities is ever-changing, says MacLaren. Items are added and deleted from the list as they are named or as new opportunities are suggested or identified. "For this reason we don't use printed materials," she says. Instead, MacLaren responds to requests for naming opportunities personally by phone or letter.

"When someone calls, I ask them about the person they would like to pay tribute to and try to match a naming opportunity with one that the donor thinks is appropriate as well as something that we need," she says.

The benefit of a naming opportunity is its prominence among other named gifts, says MacLaren. "Items are priced according to the value of the recognition rather than the cost of the item," she says. "If the item is one of many, it costs less. If it is unique, it costs more.

"Visibility also plays a factor in the cost of a particular naming opportunity."

Source: Wendy MacLaren, Vice President of Institutional Advancement, Cottey College, Nevada, MO. Phone (417) 667-8181. E-mail: wmaclaren@cottey.edu

Library Shares Naming Opportunities In Walk-Through Format

Many donors participated in naming opportunities at Thomas Crane Public Library, helping raise funds towards the construction of the 35,000-square-foot addition to their library.

Jane Granstrom, the library's assistant director, says rather than prioritizing naming opportunities based on dollar amounts, they presented them as if a person were entering through the main entrance on the lower level and touring the building one floor at a time. "This presents a variety of needs and a range of prices," says Granstrom.

To determine what amounts to ask for each, says Granstrom, they contacted libraries with new buildings or additions and product vendors to see what each cost.

Source: Jane Granstrom, Assistant Director, Thomas Crane Public Library, 40 Washington Street, Quincy, MA 02269. Phone (617) 376-1300.

IDENTIFYING NAMING OPPORTUNITIES

Named Sponsorship Opportunities

Named sponsorships differ from other named gifts in that sponsorships are generally for a specified period of time.

While many sponsorships are provided by businesses, corporations and foundations, individuals may also choose to sponsor a program or event. Even facilities are being named in honor of sponsorship support these days; however, the period of sponsorship is agreed to in advance and finite.

Although there are obvious differences between named gifts and sponsorships, they both provide a multitude of possibilities.

Below are several examples of named sponsorship opportunities:

Special Events —
- Concerts
- Athletic events
- Lectures
- Art and photo exhibits
- Fundraising events
- Outreach receptions

Special Programs —
- Camps
- Workshops
- Training sessions
- Public awareness efforts
- Community volunteer projects
- Special outreach projects
- Educational workshops
- Video or documentary production
- Special tours

Publications & Advertising:
"This publication made possible by"or
"This message brought to you by" —
- Annual reports
- Campaign literature
- Magazines/newsletters
- Manuals
- Outdoor advertising
- Television/radio commercials
- Newspaper ads
- Web sites

Consider Less Pricey Naming Gifts, Too

As much as we would prefer all million-dollar naming gifts, there are reasons why you should offer far less expensive naming gifts as well. A $1,000 naming gift from a non-donor, for example, may be what's necessary to establish a relationship with a new donor. And that relationship may turn into a larger naming gift down the road.

Here are some inexpensive naming gift opportunities that could run anywhere from $100 to $10,000:

- Bricks in the walkway or wall.
- Seats (theater, auditorium).
- Rooms (residence hall, patient).
- Desks, computers and more.

Named Equipment and Furnishings Opportunities

Though you may think the idea of named equipment as rather undramatic and unappealing, there are situations in which a particular piece of equipment can make a tremendous impact on the services an organization can provide its clients, students, patients, visitors or others. A lifesaving piece of equipment at a hospital, for instance, may have attraction to some would-be donors.

If attaching their name to that equipment is practical and helps solidify the gift commitment, why not do so?

Here is a small sampling of naming gift opportunities for equipment:

- Special medical equipment
- Special research equipment
- Musical instruments
- Furnishings within rooms
- Equipment to accommodate persons with special needs

- Special playground equipment
- Equipment for emergency needs
- Special audio/visual equipment
- Special mobile units

IDENTIFYING NAMING OPPORTUNITIES

Explore Named Room Gift Possibilities

If your organization has the luxury of having a high number of similar rooms throughout its facilities (i.e., residence hall rooms, patient rooms, etc.), a great naming opportunity lies before you.

Why not develop a plan to endow each of those rooms by allowing them to be named? Think of it. By naming each room with sufficiently large endowment gifts, the rooms' future maintenance and enhancement costs could be underwritten permanently.

Here's a simple step-by-step procedure to get the program under way:

1. Count up the number of available rooms that could be named or endowed within each building.

2. Do some budget research to estimate the annual maintenance costs associated with all of the rooms within each facility. Also take into consideration the building's age, any deferred maintenance and long-term plans for the building.

3. Determine estimated costs of any refurbishing that could be done to each room (i.e., painting/wallpapering, floor covering, window treatments, furniture replacement, etc.).

4. Based on your estimates for yearly maintenance costs and possible enhancement costs (on a per-room basis), you can calculate how much of an endowment would be necessary to provide a certain yearly expenditure amount per room. For example, if you estimate that it would take, on average, $800 per year per room, you would need to have an endowment of not less than $20,000 assuming the fund had an annual return of 4 percent ($20,000 multiplied by 4 percent equals $800.)

5. Taking both estimated costs and the fundability factor — how much a person would be willing to give to have his/her name on the room — into consideration, you can come up with a dollar amount that is reasonable to endow and name each room.

Consider the endowment potential with a room-naming program based on the total rooms you have that could be named through endowed gifts.

Although a named room may not demand the "price" of a larger space, often times there are many of them.

Named Facilities Opportunities

Entire facilities can be named for the right gift amount. In addition, portions of facilities can be named. Example: The John F. Wilcox Recreational Center might cover an entire complex while other names may be attached to separate structures/areas that are a part of the Center — gymnasium, swimming pool facility, tennis court/handball court area, etc.

It's important not to set the cost of a named building too low. The gift size associated with naming a facility will set a precedent for all other structures to be named as well as the spaces within a structure. After all, you can always "lower the price tag" if, after time, you have no takers.

Do a comparative study of other named buildings within your community and at institutions or agencies similar to yours in other communities to gauge naming gift levels.

Individual Buildings and Complexes —

- Administration building
- Athletic facility
- Museum
- Art center
- Research facility
- Hospital
- Classroom buildings
- Residential facilities
- Patient-designated buildings
- Parking structures
- Student center/commons
- Dining hall
- Zoo buildings
- Satellite facilities
- Concert hall
- Nature center
- Science building

- Fraternities and sororities
- Medical office buildings
- Maintenance facility
- Chapel
- Library
- Educational facility
- Observatory
- Youth center
- School buildings
- Planetarium
- Landmark structures
- Child care facility
- Retirement center buildings
- Camp buildings
- Recreational facilities
- Rehabilitation center
- Visitor's center

IDENTIFYING NAMING OPPORTUNITIES

Named Endowment Opportunities

Are you sharing the many types of name endowments persons may choose to establish? Here is a sampling of named endowment ideas you may wish to add to your list of possibilities.

— Personnel —

- CEO's position
- Individual faculty chairs
- Physicians' positions
- Branch center managers
- Visiting lecturers
- Nursing positions
- Development positions

- Researchers
- Counseling positions
- Branch center managers
- Activities director
- Clergy/Chaplain endowment
- Docent endowment
- Support staff endowment

— Programs —

- Outreach programs
- Volunteer programs
- Programs for senior citizens
- Wellness programs
- Gender-based programs
- Travel programs
- Educational programs
- Field trip programs
- Speakers' programs
- Mentorship endowment
- Workshops endowment
- Cultural enhancement endowment — to provide cultural opportunities

Scholarships

- Student scholarships
- Camp scholarships
- Music scholarships
- Athletic scholarships
- Continuing education
- Travel scholarships
- Internships
- Minority scholarship
- Individual health funds

— Miscellaneous —

- Publications (i.e. annual report brochures, news-letters, directories, manuals, ect.)
- Acquisitions (artwork, museum artifacts, equipment, etc.)
- Furnishings (i.e., repair/replace existing furnishings)
- Professional Development (to provide enrichment for staff)
- Outsourcet (i.e., consultants, architects, telemarketing firms, freelance writers and more)

- Public awareness to under-write costs that make public more aware of services
- Transportation or vehicle replacement
- Venture Capital (test new program ventures)
- Awards or recognition

— Facilities —

In addition to gifts large enough to name facilities, as well as spaces within and outside of facilities, any of these projects can be endowed as well. Annual interest from such named endowed funds can be used to underwrite ongoing maintenance costs and provide for renovations and long-term enhancements.

Named Endowments Focus on Outreach

If your services go beyond the community in which your organization resides, what are you doing to encourage major gifts from those geographically distant individuals and businesses?

People like giving at home, so why not establish endowment gift opportunities that allow donors to do that while still benefiting your nonprofit?

Explore offering named endowment gifts that address your nonprofit's outreach efforts. If, for instance, you represent a college or university with satellite campuses, offer named scholarships that benefit students attending a branch location. Or if your hospital provides services to neighboring communities, offer endowment gift opportunities that benefit the residents of those communities.

DETERMINING NAMING GIFT REQUIREMENTS, PRICE

How much should it cost to name a room or a building or a particular endowed fund? Whatever you decide up front will set a precedent for naming gifts that follow, so it's important to put thought into appropriate amounts for each type of naming gift. There are some formuli you can use as guides, but keep in mind they are only that: guides to be used in conjuction with other criteria.

What to Ask For Regarding Naming Rights

Q. *"Major donor prospects are questioning how we came up with amounts for naming opportunities. We based them on what we felt donors might be willing to pay. What's a more scientific method to use for future naming opportunities?"*

Marc Saffren, founder and managing director of m3 Development (Manorville, NY), recommends organizations base the cost for naming a building or spaces within a building on 20 percent of the cost of constructing the building or space.

For example, Saffren says, if a 40,000-square-foot building will cost $300 per square foot, for a total cost of $12 million, the cost for naming the building should be 20 percent of $12 million, or $2.4 million.

To get these figures, he says, sit down with your architect and general contractor: "Your architect and general contractor know the real costs of construction. They can also sometimes identify potential naming opportunities you hadn't considered."

When asked how you came up with the amounts for your naming opportunities, you can say that you consulted with your architect and your general contractor and based your naming opportunity amounts on 20 percent of the total cost of each project, which is a better answer than that you based it on what felt good to you, or what you thought was a good amount, he says.

Source: Marc S. Saffren, Founder, Managing Director, m3 Development, Manorville, NY. Phone (631) 697-3577. E-mail: msaffren@m3development.net

How to Determine Naming Gift Requirements

Texas Christian University's naming policy requires the donor to make a gift equal to at least half the cost of the project. "For capital projects, that would be half of total cost, not just construction," says Dennis Alexander, director of foundation relations.

Donors who make lesser gifts generally have parts of the building named for them, says Alexander: "As part of our fundraising plan for any building, we generally mark up a floor plan with naming gift values for every room, section or wing of the structure (except for utility, maintenance and support spaces)."

Here's the formula they use to determine the amount of each naming opportunity:

Total cost = site preparation + professional services + construction + equipment/furnishings + contingency (10 percent of construction) + maintenance endowment ($5/square foot).

"For programs, the naming donor should give an endowment sufficient to fund at least half the program's current operating budget," says Alexander. "For example, a donor who wishes to name the College of Science & Engineering must create an endowment that annually funds at least half the college operating budget."

Source: Dennis Alexander, Director of Foundation Relations, Texas Christian University, Fort Worth, TX. Phone (817) 257-5047. E-mail: D.Alexander@tcu.edu

Factors That Add to Naming Gift Appeal

As you work to find the right match between prospects and naming opportunities, keep in mind these factors that add to the appeal of certain naming gifts:

✓ The level of visibility they provide to the public.

✓ Their uniqueness.

✓ The price tag associated with naming opportunities.

✓ Their degree of singularity.

✓ The impact such gifts will have on your organization and its reputation.

✓ The impact such gifts will have on those served by your organization.

✓ The degree to which they will positively impact public perception.

✓ Their perceived longevity.

DETERMINING NAMING GIFT REQUIREMENTS, PRICE

The Science of Setting a Building's Price Tag

When considering what price to place on a naming opportunity for a new or existing facility, begin by looking at what other benchmark nonprofits are requiring for naming opportunities and what your market can bear.

Before an amount is decided upon, several discussions need to take place between your CEO and key advancement staff members. Once an agreement is reached, your board needs to buy into and approve the decision. That board-approved decision should then become a part of your organization's naming gifts policy.

Your naming gifts policy should clarify any questions or issues that may arise. For example, if a significant portion of a building is to be funded through private gifts, you may decide on a minimum percent required to name the facility. If the building cost is $15 million, for instance, and 50 percent of the cost is required to name the facility, the naming gift must be $7.5 million.

And if an entire building is being paid for with state funds, the naming gift should be set at a much lower amount. Those naming gift funds won't be used to pay for bricks and mortar projects, but can be placed into an endowment to cover future maintenance costs and to benefit the programs housed in the facility. Also, these minimum naming percentages can be adjusted upward or downward depending on the location and prestige of the building, along with other factors.

> ### Rule of Thumb
>
> As one of many guidelines you can use, figure that one-half to one-third of the cost of a building project is needed as a private gift to name it.

Naming Buildings: Use Guidelines, Not Rules

When considering the cost of naming buildings, look at each project individually, says Michael J. Catillaz, vice president for institutional advancement for Hobart & William Smith College (Geneva, NY). The college's current guideline for naming buildings is that the gift be no less than 40 percent of the building cost. "This means that we wouldn't name a building for less than 40 percent, but that some projects might require a naming gift that is greater than 40 percent," Catillaz says.

When you're raising money to build a building, he says, there are often naming opportunities available other than the building itself (i.e., lobbies, classrooms, media rooms, benches, etc.). The cost of naming the building then, he says, would depend on the college's potential to raise money based on the existence of other naming opportunities and a donor base to support them.

"For example, we're raising money to build a building for Studio Arts," he says. "The building will have huge, open lighted areas, with few separate rooms. There will be almost no naming opportunities other than the building itself. If we allowed a donor to name that building for 40 percent, we would still have to raise the other 60 percent with no other naming opportunities available. There are also endowment provisions to be considered. For that building, we will ask for a greater overall percentage of the building to name it."

Source: Michael J. Catillaz, Vice President for Institutional Advancement, Hobart & William Smith College, Geneva, NY. Phone (315) 781-3535.

> ### Set Standards for Smaller Naming Opportunities
>
> While the cost to name a building should be looked at on a case-by-case basis, smaller naming opportunities that go along with it should follow specific standards, says Michael J. Catillaz, vice president for institutional advancement for Hobart & William Smith College (Geneva, NY). Smaller naming opportunities could include benches, classrooms or lobbies.
>
> "The setting of naming gifts for comparable spaces across an organization needs to be made in consideration of the importance of the precedence it will set," Catillaz says.
>
> For example, you don't want to let a donor put his name on a classroom for $50,000 one day, and then ask another donor to name a classroom for $250,000 at a later date, he says. "Additionally, modest naming levels can frequently lower the sights of donors who might otherwise make a more significant contribution."

DETERMINING NAMING GIFT REQUIREMENTS, PRICE

A Great Solution to Underpriced Naming Gift Opportunities

Officials with The Oregon Symphony Orchestra realized a few years into their endowment program that they were underpricing their named endowed chair and program opportunities. They had offered naming opportunities in recognition of large gifts to the symphony's Centennial Campaign, but in reality, those gifts weren't large enough to cover the real costs of those chairs, says Leslie Tuomi, director of major gifts and foundations.

As a result, they revamped their naming figures to be more in line with what was needed to fund a program.

"We worried that prospects would find the new figures too high, so we decided to offer them a few choices," Tuomi says. Donors can now name a chair or program in perpetuity, or for 10, five or three years, all for different prices. A Principal Chair, for example, can be named in perpetuity for $1.5 million, for 10 years for $750,000, for five years for $375,000 and for three years for $225,000.

In addition to offering donors more choices, the new naming levels have another benefit, says Tuomi: "If someone names a chair or program for a shorter period, there is always the opportunity to ask them to extend the naming period by making another gift."

Source: Leslie Tuomi, Director of Major Gifts & Foundations, Oregon Symphony Orchestra, Portland, OR.. Phone (503) 228-4294. E-mail: ltuomi@orsymphony.org

By giving would-be donors more choices it allows them to donate at a level they feel comfortable doing.

Offer Varying Endowment Thresholds

The amount of money required to establish a named endowment should be determined by:

1. What that fund will be expected to accomplish — its impact.

2. The visibility the fund will generate in relation to other funds.

Your nonprofit's age, size of your constituency and historical giving will also play into setting threshold amounts for various types of endowments.

The key is to offer a variety of endowment opportunities with varying thresholds to give everyone a choice. Not everyone can afford to endow a faculty chair with a threshold of $1 million, nor does a faculty chair appeal to everyone.

Develop a menu of naming endowment opportunities, such as the example shown here, to include in handouts and promote on your website.

Minimum Endowment Levels

This list represents a sampling of naming gift endowments you can establish. Minimum gift levels to create various types of endowments have been set to guarantee income will be adequate to achieve the benefactor's vision, now and in the future. Gifts may be added later to build the endowment over time.

Endowment Type	Threshold Required
Building	$5,000,000*
Departmental Endowment	$3,000,000
Chair	$1,000,000
Lectureship	$500,000
Equipment Fund	$500,000
Visiting Professor	$250,000
Program Endowment	$100,000*
Office Endowment	$50,000*
Book Fund	$25,000
Internship	$25,000
Recognition Award/Prize	$25,000
Scholarship	$25,000
Auditorium Seating	$5,000

Thresholds Vary

Endowments may be established with less than threshold amounts; however, the threshold should be reached within a reasonable amount of time.

Marketing Endowment

Don't hesitate to include a chart in printed materials comparing your current endowment with the endowments of those institutions to whom you aspire.

INTRODUCING, CLOSING NAMED GIFTS

Although no two donors nor naming opportunities are alike, there are procedures you can follow when introducing the idea of a naming gift, cultivating a naming gift and soliciting a gift. Each "move" on your part should build the foundation for moves that follow and lead toward the realization of a major named gift.

When Naming Opportunities Enter Into the Discussion

When do naming opportunities enter into the major gift discussion?

For some organizations, this doesn't happen until after the gift amount has been negotiated. A separate gift committee considers a particular naming opportunity before making a recommendation to the board chair or executive director.

For other organizations, the discussion of naming opportunities begins right away, and is an integral part of the negotiations with the donor.

Maret School (Washington, DC) is one of the latter organizations. Sally Dunkelberger, the school's director of development, says the discussion of naming opportunities is done upfront and is part of the solicitation. "Naming opportunities are part of the conversation with the donor," Dunkelberger says. "We include a pre-authorized list of naming opportunities and amounts as part of our campaign packet."

Maret's policy is that at least $50,000 of a multi-year pledge needs to be paid within 12 months of the pledge to reserve a naming opportunity, she adds. "We won't put the plaques on the walls until the entire pledge has been paid."

Source: Sally Dunkelberger, Director of Development, Maret School, 3000 Cathedral Ave., NW, Washington DC 20008. Phone: (202) 939-8800.
E-mail: sdunkelberger@maret.org

Clarify 'Naming Rights' When Speaking With Donors

Do your volunteers, staff, donors and sponsors understand the term "naming rights"?

To avoid confusion when talking to staff, donors and volunteers, Terry Burton, president, Dig In Research 2007 Inc. (Vancouver, British Columbia, Canada) recommends distinguishing between the two types of naming rights agreements.

Burton defines the two categories as:

❑ **Naming Rights PH —**
This label can be used to identify a philanthropic gift that was recognized by the nonprofit with the granting of naming rights. These nonprofits may confer naming rights to a donor in appreciation of a major gift. In this case, the naming rights refer to the recognition bestowed upon the individual, corporation, foundation or other funding agency that made a gift. It is a gift that comes with no hooks attached or additional expectations from the donor over and above the usual name recognition that is the custom of the organization.

❑ **Naming Rights SP —**
This type refers to sponsorships and can be found in the private sector, nonprofit sector, municipalities and government organizations. "These are financial agreements to name a property in exchange for a specified amount of

money for a stated period of time," says Burton. He says an interesting trend rising from this category has been acquisition of naming rights from nonprofits, school boards and other groups outside the private sector by private sector companies: "The acquisition of these naming rights are all about building and enhancing brand names, and not philanthropy or charitable support."

Source: Terry Burton, President, Dig In Research 2007 Inc., Vancouver, British Columbia, Canada. Phone (604) 801-5107. E-mail: tburton@diginresearch.biz

Don't Leave Key People Out of Naming Decisions

When it comes to naming gifts, it's important to be inclusive. Make a point to invite spouses and even children of donors, if appropriate, in selecting the appropriate name to be used. Rather than limit involvement of others, let the donors make the decision not to involve someone in making naming gift decisions.

Granted, more heads may make the selection of a named gift more cumbersome. However, anyone who becomes involved will take greater ownership of the named gift and your pool of would-be donors will expand based on their engagement in the entire process.

Once the gift has been given, continue to steward all persons who were involved in the gift in any way.

INTRODUCING, CLOSING NAMED GIFTS

Help Prospects Explore Various Naming Possibilities

As you work with prospects on various funding projects, it will be helpful to illustrate a wide variety of naming gift possibilities so they can select one that best meets their goals and desires.

Beyond using the donor's own name, he/she can choose from among these in honor or in memory possibilities:

* Parents of the donor
* Grandparents of the donor
* Donor's spouse
* Company name
* Mentor
* National hero
* Children of the donor
* Name combination (i.e. Smith/Harken)
* Community, state or regional name
* Someone associated with your organization (i.e., founding member, respected employee)
* Religious figure
* Celebrity or public servant
* Someone served by your organization (i.e., former patient, a victim, student)

Multiple naming possibilities also encourages additional future naming gifts.

Using a form like the one shown below will help prospects see all naming possiblities.

Use Form to Assist Donors' Naming Efforts

How much support do you offer donors as they weigh what to call a newly endowed scholarship, a newly launched program or renovated space in a building? Do you simply throw out a couple of possibilities or do you guide them through a process that will make them more fully satisfied with their final decision?

Make use of a naming considerations form (such as the one shown below) that can aid donors in selecting their top choice for a named gift. Meet with those involved to point out various naming possibilities, then encourage them to take some time to weigh those possibilities before making a final decision.

Naming Considerations Form

As you weigh naming possibilities for your gift, recognize the many choices that are available to you. Your gift could be named in honor or memory of:_____

❑ Parent	❑ Mentor	❑ Yourself
❑ Child	❑ Business	❑ Spouse
❑ Other family	❑ A place	❑ Business associate
❑ Other		

Once you have selected a name (or combination of names), give thought to the manner in which you would prefer to have the name(s) listed:

Last name only:	The Walsh Fund
Combination of names:	The Michael and Kate Walsh Fund
	The Walsh/Lester Fund
Inclusion of maiden names:	The Susan Shaw Walsh Fund
Inclusion of "memorial":	The Albert Walsh Memorial Fund
Descriptive wording:	The Walsh Scholarship Fund
	Walsh Family Seminar Room

Write down naming possibilities that come to mind in the first column, then prioritize your choices in the second column:

1._____	1._____
2._____	2._____
3._____	3._____
4._____	4._____
5._____	5._____
6._____	6._____
7._____	7._____

INTRODUCING, CLOSING NAMED GIFTS

Encourage Naming Gifts That Include Mentors

The opportunity to immortalize one's self, a family member or other loved one is often a component in a named major gift. In exploring various naming opportunities, however, how often do you place donors' mentors on the table as a naming option?

Suggesting named gifts in honor of persons — outside of immediate family members — who have had an overwhelming impact on their lives. It may be perceived by some as a great way of saying thank you to admired mentors. To better market the mentor naming gift option among those who are exploring major gifts:

1. Encourage all development officers to ask probing questions about persons who most influenced a prospect's life. Include responses in call reports following prospect visits.

2. Draft an article for your charity's magazine or newsletter that suggests named gifts in honor of mentors. Even better: If you have someone who has established a named gift in honor of a mentor, include that profile as a feature article.

3. If a prospect warms to the idea of a named mentor gift, explore the possibility of actually including his/her mentor, if living, or family member, if the mentor is deceased, in discussions about the gift and its use. Who knows, the mentor or mentor's family may decide to make an investment in the fund or project as well.

Would-be donors may like the idea of naming something after a long-time mentor.

Naming Opportunity Rules

Q. "Should naming opportunities always include the donor's name, e.g., 'Lane Welcome Center,' or can you request the donor be recognized only on the plaque?"

"The most common form of naming gift recognition has been the use of the donor's name in the renamed property. The example of the 'Lane Welcome Center' is used in about 80 percent of circumstances where a nonprofit has received a major gift that will be recognized with this type of donor recognition.

"In the last few years, several other approaches have begun to appear, including naming the property using the first names of the husband and wife or partners, or the family of the multiple donors, for example, 'The Labatt Family Cancer Center,' or 'The Sacia and Jeremy Smith Recreation Complex.'

"Where there was a joint gift by a husband and wife, it has become a best practice policy to ask the donors in what order they want the name recognition to appear. Referring to the above example ... the donors would have several choices, including 'Sacia & Jeremy Smith Recreation Complex;' 'Sacia Burton & Jeremy Smith Recreation Complex' or 'Jeremy and Sacia Smith Recreation Complex.'

"From a stewardship perspective, asking the donor what works best for them is an important step in developing a meaningful relationship that extends to the family and friends of the donors.

"Name recognition on the plaque only is a donor relations strategy for smaller gifts such as indoor properties (e.g., naming a classroom, wing, auditorium or elevator). Another example of best practice policy regarding named gifts is that a gift for an indoor property is typically not given outdoor signage.

"The dollar amount spent on the signage recognition is in proportion to the dollar amount of the gift and length of term for the naming rights. Expect to budget a larger amount for in-perpetuity named gifts as compared to a named gift for a limited term such as 10 years.

"Involving the donor early in the naming process can help have long-term benefits that are unseen at the time of the naming ceremony."

— *Terry Burton, President, Dig In Research (Vancouver, British Columbia)*

When discussing possibilities for naming options, always keep donors' best interests in mind.

INTRODUCING, CLOSING NAMED GIFTS

Explore Endowment Possibilities With Your Constituents

What are you currently doing to make constituents aware of how they can make endowment gifts to your cause? Are they familiar with the possibilities that exist?

You may find a simple introductory brochure helpful for illustrating the many choices available when establishing named endowed funds. Although you may offer more detailed or customized literature later in the cultivation process, a simple piece that illustrates funding possibilities can be helpful in getting prospects to visualize themselves as major donors and also see how annual interest from their endowed funds would make a noticeable difference.

An introductory brochure such as the sample below also points out the minimum required to establish an endowed fund for your cause. Plus, it illustrates various ways in which one can fulfill a pledge, illustrating that major gifts can be affordable for many who wish to invest in your organization's long-range plans.

In addition, this format shows prospects your organization's total anticipated needs in various categories. Although donors have the option of establishing named funds for lesser amounts within a particular category, there may be those who choose to fund an entire need on their own.

Sample introductory brochure used to introduce endowment gift opportunities.

Help Ensure Our Children's Future — Establish a Named Endowment

You can make a world of difference for generations to come by establishing a named endowment fund through the Jefferson School Foundation. Annual income from your endowment will provide valuable and ongoing tools necessary to prepare Jefferson students for life's goals.

JEFFERSON SCHOOL FOUNDATION **JSF**

Although named endowment funds begin at $10,000 — since only a portion of the fund's annual interest is used to fund intended programs — donors can establish such funds over a period of time if they so choose. For example, a donor could:

- Pledge to contribute funds over an agreed-to number of years until the fund reaches a particular amount.
- Pledge to contribute funds over a number of years and then add to the fund through a planned gift.
- Make an irrevocable planned gift which will commence after the lifetime of the donor.
- Make a onetime, outright gift of $10,000 or more to fully fund a particular program or project.

Below is a small sampling of some endowment funds you may wish to consider establishing. Please keep in mind, donors may establish named funds for as little as $10,000 for any program or project even though the total needed for that program or project exceeds that amount.

Travel Fund
Total Endowment Needed: $25,000

Often students qualify to participate in some academic or extracurricular experience that requires travel but they are unable to cover associated costs - lodging, meals, transportation, entry fees,etc. This fund would help ensure that every student can participate regardless of his or her family's financial circumstances.

Technology Fund
Total Endowment Needed: $500,000
Annual interest from the establishment of this fund would allow our school to make needed computer and related equipment purchases and, equally important, provide funding to cover maintenance of such equipment.

Endowed Positions
Total Endowment Needed: $1 million

Funds established in this category would underwrites the total cost of particular positions at Jefferson - both existing or new positions. Annual interest would cover salary and benefits, and helps ensure that our school attracts top professionals from throughout the region and nation.

Post-Secondary Scholarships
Total Endowment Needed: Unlimited
Annual scholarship awards to graduating seniors will help guarantee that our graduates continue the tradition of educational preparedness they received as Jefferson students.

High School Internships
Total Endowment Needed: $50,000

Annual interest from this fund would be used to make internship more accessible to juniors and seniors during the school year as well as the summer.

Teachers' Professional Development
Total Endowment Needed: $150,000

Annual interst would be awarded to derving teachers for learning and continuing education.

Capital Improvements/Maintenance
Total Endowment Needed: $1 million

Annual interest from this category will be used for needed capital improvements to school, facilities and the grounds.

INTRODUCING, CLOSING NAMED GIFTS

Why It Pays to Identify Your Prospects' Heroes

Take a moment and reflect: Who, outside of immediate family, are your biggest heroes? Who immediately comes to mind as someone who had a tremendously positive influence on your life? If money were no object, wouldn't you relish the opportunity to establish an endowed fund or name a building in honor or in memory of one of your heroes?

That same approach can be used as you meet with prospects capable of making significant gifts. Although many will choose to establish a gift in their own names or the name of a love one, others will be motivated by the thought of making a gift in honor of one of their heroes.

As you meet with prospects, remember to ask probing questions that reveal their life's heroes. Who are these persons? Why do the prospects hold these individuals in such high esteem? How did their heroes help them or influence them in such momentous ways? Why might it be appropriate to tie the hero's name, in perpetuity, to the funding project you have in mind?

Don't underestimate the impact prospects' heroes can have in bringing about sizeable named gifts.

Encourage Employees To Establish a Naming Gift

In addition to encouraging your organization's employees to consider a naming gift, why not give them the option of making a collective gift (as a department or an entire body) to establish a naming gift in honor of someone they jointly respect: a retired employee, a famous person.

Essential Elements of a Named Gift Agreement

Before soliciting gifts of any size, be sure to have board-approved formal gift-acceptance policies, says Robert Evans, managing director, The EHL Consulting Group (Willow Grove, PA).

Such policies, Evans says, should clarify common aspects of any major gift and represent a set of procedures that would be appropriate for every gift, regardless of the level.

Be prepared also to formalize the pledge at the time a major gift is secured by developing a named gift agreement for the donor that spells out the specifics of his or her gift.

"Named gift agreements should be created by the organization, not the donor, and signed by both a representative of the organization and a representative of the donor," Evans says.

He shares essential elements all named gift agreements should include:

- Whether the gift is in perpetuity or over a fixed period of time; if over a fixed time, when the clock starts.

- What will happen if the institution moves (if it is a capital naming).

- How much of the gift must be paid before it is considered a formal gift (e.g., when name would go above the building or space; Evans suggests 60 percent).

- Payment schedule for multi-year gifts.

- If it is a capital gift, are there any restrictions on placing compatible namings within the space (e.g., if the donor is naming a gallery in a museum, would other donors be allowed to dedicate benches)?

- Whether the donor has any say regarding interior or exterior decorating of the space.

A gift agreement's tone should be friendly, says Evans, and the document should be written in clear, simple, easy-to-understand language that supports and reflects the major commitment that the donor has made to the organization.

Source: Robert Evans, Managing Director, The EHL Consulting Group, Willow Grove, PA. Phone (215) 830-0304. E-mail: revans@ehlconsulting.com

Make sure, before soliciting any named gifts, to have a formal, approved gift-accepting policy in place.

INTRODUCING, CLOSING NAMED GIFTS

Create a Naming Opportunity Agreement With Donors

Content not available in this edition

If you are in the midst of a capital campaign which will include naming opportunities, you might want to consider creating a naming opportunity agreement. This agreement would spell out issues such as how long the naming opportunity will last, what specifically is being named, and what would happen in the event the named building burns down, is rebuilt or renovated.

The New York Hall of Science's Capital Campaign Cabinet created a donor recognition policy that outlines the types of naming opportunities they offer and covers issues related to signage.

When the organization was in an expansion campaign, how namings would be created and facilitated became an issue as they identified naming possibilities to present to prospects.

In addition to a donor recognition policy (above left), cabinet members created a donor guidance form (below left) which requires the donor to sign off on the agreed-to naming opportunity. The form includes space for the official naming/signage, approval for a shortening of the name, (i.e., from the "Mary & John G. Smith Technology Gallery" to "Smith Tech Gallery") and approval for using the naming title in press releases and other printed material.

Content not available in this edition

NAMING GIFT OPPORTUNITIES: How to Successfully Secure More Naming Gifts

MARKETING TOOLS, STRATEGIES TO GAIN NAMING GIFTS

There are a variety of methods and strategies you can use to make would-be donors aware of naming gift possibilities and to "sell" those opportunities to financially-capable donors. This chapter shares a wide sampling of ideas and tools you can use to market naming gifts.

Have Your Ever Publicized Naming Opportunities?

It's one thing to produce campaign literature that talks about naming gift opportunities, but would you ever publicize them?

In a press release announcing their campaign, Saint Louis University officials mentioned that they were actively pursuing a donor to make a major gift to name their new Health Sciences Center Research building.

Paul Schnabel, associate vice president in university development for the Missouri university, says that although they were looking for a donor to make a naming gift for the building in the traditional ways, (examining current donor base to identify major donors for their school of medicine; talking with friends, trustees, key volunteers, etc. of the university to identify prospects), they thought it was important to state that finding a naming donor for this particular building was a priority.

"We are currently in the process of raising funds for two major new buildings," Schnabel says. "We wanted potential donors and friends to know that we see this building as a campaign priority."

Source: Paul Schnabel, Associate Vice President in University Development, Saint Louis University, St. Louis, MO. Phone (314) 977-2499. E-mail: schnabep@slu.edu

Don't be shy about publicizing naming gift opportunities.

Update Prospects, Donors on Naming Projects' Status

Do you publish a regular update for top prospects and donors throughout the duration of your capital campaign? Doing so is a good move. Regular updates ensure that your campaign stays in the minds of key players and serves to keep both donors and prospects aware of your fund-raising progress.

If you have a menu of naming projects for your campaign, list those opportunities in each update, indicating those that have been taken and those that still remain — not unlike newspaper real estate sections in which some homes are still for sale and some are marked "sold." Doing this subtly reminds each prospect that campaign progress is being made and that time is running out to select the naming project of his or her choice.

Showcase Naming Gift Opportunities Online

Looking for more ways to market naming gift opportunities? Why not make them available on your website?

Officials with Children's Healthcare of Atlanta (Atlanta, GA) not only provide naming gift opportunities on their website, they allow visitors to categorize those opportunities by specialty or price range.

Although visitors cannot reserve or contribute to naming opportunities on the website, they can explore naming opportunities that interest them. It's basically just for shopping, says Jane Ellington, director of donor relations.

For more information, visit: www.choa.org/campaign/NamingOpps/index.asp.

Source: Jane Ellington, Director of Donor Relations, Children's Healthcare of Atlanta, Atlanta, GA. Phone (404) 785-7336. E-mail: jane.ellington@choa.org

Use today's high-tech world to help market your gift options.

MARKETING TOOLS, STRATEGIES TO GAIN NAMING GIFTS

Revise Strategy for Major Gifts, Naming Opportunities

How often do you review your organization's strategy for asking for major gifts naming opportunities?

With the dramatic change in the economy, nonprofits should consider making adjustments, says Terry Burton, president, Dig In Research 2007 Inc. (Vancouver, British Columbia, Canada).

Burton offers suggestions to assist in adjusting your major gift strategy with regard to naming opportunities:

1. **Change length of time to name a property.** More than 90 percent of nonprofits use a one-dimensional approach for named gifts by naming a property or endowment in perpetuity. Burton says a growing number of nonprofits use a multi-year strategy that offers donors a choice and broadens the discussion with a major gift prospect. Consider offering three-, five-, 10- or 20-year periods for a named gift, plus an option to name in perpetuity.

2. **Revisit ask amounts of naming opportunities.** If you have not done this recently, chances are your amounts are not relevant in today's marketplace.

3. **Consider taking naming opportunities off the market.** "This tactic will buy your organization time," says Burton. "Naming opportunities are precious commodities and in short supply. If the market has changed dramatically, take dramatic action."

4. **Revise major gifts strategy.** Be patient. The market will change again. Use this time to revise your strategy for major gifts by thinking about what is currently on the market and what is not. From endowments to bricks and mortar, review your inventory of what has been marketed to major gift prospects.

5. **Use variable pricing strategy.** This allows nonprofits to offer naming opportunities at one amount for a cash gift and a larger dollar amount for a planned gift.

6. **Consider benchmarking.** This tactic can have a positive impact in uncertain financial times. "Benchmarking can help to revise your own strategy in a short amount of time," says Burton. "If you go this route, think carefully before you publish your revised list. Try to take the emotion out of accepting a major gift for a high-profile property."

7. **Consider two-tier pricing system.** This would include one philanthropic gift and a second, higher ask amount for a corporate sponsorship of the same property. The cost of stewardship for a corporate sponsorship is higher than for a philanthropic gift for the same property, Burton says. Over the long term, the nonprofit winds up subsidizing the corporate sponsor because of expectations that come from signing a naming rights agreement. Now is a good time to make a fundamental change in the length of term for a named gift and how much it costs to closely link to your organization.

Source: Terry Burton, President, Dig In Research 2007 Inc., Vancouver, British Columbia, Canada. Phone (604) 801-5107. E-mail: tburton@diginresearch.biz

Shift Fundraising Focus

In today's economy, nonprofits must implement a new fundraising model to succeed, says Terry Burton, president, Dig In Research 2007 Inc. (Vancouver, British Columbia, Canada).

That new model should include:

✓ **Engaging the community through stewardship.** Think about a larger group than just your past donors. Consider extending your stewardship message to people and organizations that have not supported you before. Talk about accountability and impact of previous major gifts.

✓ **Review of naming policy.** Burton says chances are it was developed at a time very different from today. "As the private sector undergoes scrutiny and change, you should expect the same from major gift donors and prospects."

✓ **Invitation to see what you do without being asked for a gift;** earning the right to be considered for a major gift.

✓ **Sharing the process of change.** Make others outside your organization aware of the process of change your organization is undertaking and what adjustments you have made to ask amounts.

MARKETING TOOLS, STRATEGIES TO GAIN NAMING GIFTS

Share Lists of Naming Gift Opportunities With Would-Be Donors

Share a list of naming opportunities and corresponding gift amounts when meeting with would-be donors.

In meeting with would-be donors, having a visual menu of naming gift opportunities — and corresponding gift minimums — allows them to select an option that is both appealing and affordable. Donors can compare naming opportunities based on their interests, the prestige associated with each option and more.

Producing a comparative list of naming gift opportunities also forces staff to prioritize the prices associated with each opportunity before the publication goes to print. It helps to solidify everyone's final decision.

The development officer can walk through each naming gift opportunity when meeting with a prospect and then leave the list for the donor to study further.

Below is a sample of a handout listing naming gift opportunities and their corresponding minimum price tags.

XYZ COLLEGE — A CAPITAL ACHIEVEMENT
SELECTED NAMING GIFT OPPORTUNITIES

Selected naming gift opportunities have been established for the Campaign. Funding amounts listed are minimums.

For details on specific funding projects, please contact The Office of College Advancement: 800-111-1111.

FACULTY SUPPORT NAMING OPPORTUNITY	MINIMUM FUNDING
Endow a deanship	$3 million or more
Endow a directorship or departmental chair	$2 million or more
Endow a faculty chair	$1 million
Endow a professorship	$500,000
Endow a faculty research fund	$250,000
Endow a visiting professorship	$250,000
Endow a lectureship	$100,000

SUPPORT FOR STUDENT NAMING OPPORTUNITIES	MINIMUM FUNDING
Endow a Graduate Student Fellowship	$100,000
Endow an Undergraduate Scholarship	$10,000

SUPPORT FOR PROGRAM AND FACILITIES NAMING OPPORTUNITY	MINIMUM FUNDING
Name a school	$10 million
Name a new or renovated building	One half construction cost
Name a research center or academic program	$1 million or more
Endow a campus library	$1 million or more
Endow a laboratory	$1 million
Endow a classroom	$500,000
Establish an endowed collection fund	$10,000

MARKETING TOOLS, STRATEGIES TO GAIN NAMING GIFTS

Seven Strategies for Selling Named Bricks

Whether you're just beginning a brick campaign or your current one has stalled, Meghan Marsden, director of the annual fund for Northern Illinois University (Dekalb, IL), shares some successful strategies to give your brick selling a jump start:

1. Stuff brochures into the receipts of donors who gave to something other than the project which the bricks benefit.

2. Use e-mail to alumni and faculty and staff. Set up a page on your website where alumni and friends can purchase a brick online. See NIU's: www.niufoundation.org/buyabrick

3. Offer payroll deduction to faculty and staff.

4. Create a traveling display you can take to events to spread the word.

5. Advertise the bricks and the website in your alumni magazine, newsletter, etc.

6. Reach out to the community with a press release that lists the campaign website.

7. Send a mailing to those who have made previous memorial gifts; bricks are a great way to honor someone.

Source: Meghan M. Marsden, Director of the Annual Fund, Northern Illinois University, Dekalb, IL. Phone (815) 753-6560. E-mail: B70MMM1@wpo.cso.niu.edu

You can generate significant dollars with a name a brick program.

Create a Naming Opportunities Brochure

The Andrew Young School of Policy Studies at Georgia State University (Atlanta, GA), uses a naming opportunity brochure on major gift calls with individuals. "It's a good conversation starter for donors, and they can refer to it once we leave," says Bill Doerr, development director.

The six-panel, full-color brochure lists naming gift levels for specific floors, centers, programs and chairs. The brochure invites prospects to assume a leadership role through their contribution.

To signify that a naming opportunity was taken prior to the printing of the brochure, the dollar amount is replaced with "NAMED." The brochure is reprinted once the majority of items are sold. It can be reviewed at: http://aysps.gsu.edu/new/naming_brochure.pdf

The Friends of the Minneapolis Public Library employs a similar document primarily for internal purposes — as a guide to donor recognition opportunities approved by library trustees. "We rarely use the document in discussions with donors.," says Colin Hamilton, executive direcetor of The Friends of the Minneapolis Public Library. "We don't want our donors to become excited over lower level gift options before we have a chance to present higher levels more suited to their interests."

The word "named" is also placed next to donor commitments. "This helps eliminate confusion over available opportunities, while demonstrating active donor participation," Hamilton explains.

Useful Marketing Tool

To help promote naming gifts, create a brochure that lists and describes all existing named gifts: endowment, physical spaces, etc.

Give a brief description of how each named gift was used along with a brief bio of the donor(s).

In addition to encouraging named gifts, the piece also serves to recognize existing donors.

Source: Bill Doerr, Development Director, Andrew Young School of Policy Studies, Georgia State University, Atlanta, GA. Phone (401) 413-0009. E-mail: billdoerr@gsu.edu
Colin Hamilton, Executive Director, The Friends of the Minneapolis Public Library, Minneapolis, MN. Phone (612) 630-6170. E-mail: cjhamilton@mplib.org

MARKETING TOOLS, STRATEGIES TO GAIN NAMING GIFTS

Launch a Buy-a-Seat Campaign

If your organization is planning an expansion, renovation or addition that features classrooms, an auditorium or other mass-seating arena, consider selling seat sponsorships.

Staff and supporters of Capitol Theatre (Rome, NY) launched the Capitol Theatre Buy-a-Seat Program in May 2008 as part of ongoing efforts to restore the historic theatre.

The program offers a lower-cost naming rights opportunity to raise money for the theatre's restoration fund, the first priority of which is restoring its 1928 blade and marquee, says Kylie Pierce, development coordinator.

All of the theatre's 1,788 seats are being sold. Prices range from $100 for second-level balcony seats to $500 for front and center seats on the lower level and balcony. A variety of seats between those areas are available for $250.

Names of donors are featured on armrest plaques.

"Seat sales have been a fairly small part of our overall fundraising efforts," Pierce says. "We will link the official kick-off of our Buy-a-Seat program to the start of our capital campaign, which is one to two years away."

In time for the official campaign kick-off, they will offer more perks to seat purchasers, she says, including movie nights and special sit-in-your-seat events.

They promote the program in onscreen notices, a brochure and newsletter, and plan to do so on their website, as well as seek other ways to get the word out.

Source: Kylie Pierce, Development Coordinator, Capitol Theatre, Rome, NY. Phone (315) 337-6277. E-mail: agirlnamedkylie@yahoo.com

Content not available in this edition

Excuse Me, But You're In My Seat....

Persons who participate in the seat-naming campaign for the Vital Express Center for the Performing Arts (Santa Clarita, CA) get more than a name plaque on a seat — they get the opportunity to purchase season tickets for those seats before the box office opens to the public. The perk is helping sell more named seats and event tickets.

A few weeks before tickets go on sale at the box office, Cathy Ritz, College of the Canyons Foundation director of development, sends a letter and form asking named-seat donors if they'd like to buy season tickets for their seats. If they choose not to do so, they can purchase tickets through the box office when it opens, but are not guaranteed those tickets will be for their named seats.

Ritz says that while most organizations that do seat-naming campaigns don't allow donors to reserve their named seats, her organization does so to offer more recognition than just a plaque.

"We have the process down to a fine art," she says. "With only 920 seats in our theater, it's manageable to offer seat donors an opportunity to sit in their own seats. It has definitely helped us sell far more seats."

Ritz says she mails the letters early enough so donors can return their forms prior to the sales opening to the public. She also calls the persons who have named seats to confirm that they received the letter and to reiterate the offer.

"I don't want anyone to claim that they didn't receive the information and be disappointed that they missed out on the opportunity," Ritz says.

Source: Cathy Ritz, Director of Development, College of the Canyons Center for Performing Arts, Santa Clarita, CA. Phone (661) 362-3639. E-mail: cathy.ritz@canyons.edu

Use unique perks to entice would-be donors to participate in your campaign.

MARKETING TOOLS, STRATEGIES TO GAIN NAMING GIFTS

Develop a Campaign to Name a Room

Looking to grow your endowment? How about a name-that-room campaign?

Whether you have dormitory rooms, patient rooms, employee offices, activity or other types of rooms, this method allows you to secure sizeable endowment gifts in return for naming rights.

Decide on the minimum dollar amount it will take to name your smallest rooms, (say $25,000), and assign increasingly higher amounts to larger, more prestigious rooms. Annual income generated from each named fund will underwrite maintenance and improvements to those rooms or offices.

Create Compelling Marketing Pieces

The Kappa Alpha Order Educational Foundation (Lexington, VA) developed a six-page, full-color brochure to highlight their naming opportunities during their capital campaign.

The brochure outlined the size and type of gifts that would receive naming opportunities and the recognition that donors would receive. It also listed all of the foundation's naming opportunities, divided into giving levels based on the foundation's giving clubs. Gifts of $500,000 and above, for example, were listed in The Robert E. Lee Circle section, and gifts of $250,000 to $499,999, were listed in the George C. Marshall Society section.

"Naming opportunities brochures should include a comprehensive listing of your naming opportunities and all amounts available," says Larry Stanton Wiese, executive director. "It should also include pledge fulfillment terms, such as whether or not estate gifts can be used to reserve a naming opportunity."

It is important to offer a variety of different naming opportunities, he says, since some donors will prefer a typical bricks and mortar naming opportunity, while others will prefer a named scholarship or an endowment/program naming opportunity.

The Foundation's naming opportunities brochure was posted as a downloadable PDF on their website (www.kaoef.org/pdf/gift_opportunities_6x9.pdf). It was also featured in their quarterly magazine and foundation annual report consistently during the campaign, mailed to donors and prospects, and given to donors and prospects by development staff during face-to-face meetings, says Stanton Wiese.

Source: Larry Stanton Wiese, Executive Director, Kappa Alpha Order and the Kappa Alpha Order Educational Foundation, Lexington, VA. Phone (540) 463-1865 x. 2001. E-mail: lswiese@ka-order.org

To help would-be donors take a more in-depth look at your naming opportunities, develop a comprehensive brochure highlighting the various aspects of your naming gifts and the impact they will have on your organization and those you serve.

Content not available in this edition

CREATING MEMORIAL, IN TRIBUTE GIFTS

Both memorial and in-tribute gifts can be used as ways to establish naming gifts in honor or in memory of special people in donors' lives: a spouse, a parent, a child, a mentor, a great leader and more. Explore all of the ways in which you can help friends of your organization establish naming funds in honor or in memory of someone.

Step-by-step Guide for Creating a Named Fund

Follow this step-by-step procedure to help donors set up a named memorial or in-tribute gift.

Anniversary dates, retirements and even deaths present opportunities to honor a person or program that has made a positive impact on your organization, says Mari Sue Johnson, director of donor relations, Willamette University (Salem, OR).

Willamette staff recently took advantage of the biology department's 100th anniversary to honor the memory of a longtime professor by creating the Donald Breakey Biology Centennial Scholarship.

To create a named fund, Johnson says to:

1. Identify a person or program to honor.
2. Identify staff to manage solicitation.
3. Identify key volunteers to lead or participate in the solicitation.
4. Write a summary of why the fund is to be established and a brief case for support.
5. Document the purpose of the fund, programs the fund will support and in the case of a scholarship, the award criteria.
6. Determine the minimum goal to endow the fund.
7. Establish a time line with actions and an end date to reach the goal.

Johnson says to identify and contact lead donors before soliciting funds from the community. If you are unable to identify lead donors, you will know immediately that timing is not right for this particular fund.

With initial funds secured, begin marketing and soliciting funds by:

- Introducing the new fund through an article in your regular publications.
- Selecting a target audience for a direct appeal. Send mailings and ask volunteers to make personal calls. Additionally, she says, the new fund will also serve as an excellent entrée for your development officers to start discussions with potential donors.
- Continuing to showcase the fund with updates in your publications.
- Printing a final report thanking all donors, at the end of the campaign.

Source: Mari Sue Johnson, Director of Donor Relations, Willamette University, Salem, OR. Phone (503) 370-6740. E-mail: mjohnson@willamette.edu

CREATING MEMORIAL, IN TRIBUTE GIFTS

Timing and Tact Are Key to Establishing Named Memorials

Don't underestimate the importance of exploring major gift opportunities — or at least planting the seed — during the loss of a loved one.

It goes without saying that it's important to use a great deal of tact in determining if and when you should broach the subject of a memorial with the deceased's loved ones. However, it is very appropriate to at least outline the options available when family members come to you or publicly announce that memorial gifts may be directed to your charity. When that does occur, follow these guidelines:

The passing of a loved one is often an appropriate time to approach a prospective donor about a named memorial gift.

1. **Cover procedures for handling memorial gifts as soon as you are notified.** Explain that all memorial gifts directed to your charity will be placed in a holding account until a later date when you and the appropriate family members can meet to determine how the gifts will be used. Also inform the family that, in addition to sending donors a note of thanks, you will provide the family with the names and addresses of all contributors.

2. **Be sure your charity is well-represented at the funeral and wake.** If your charity has been or might be named a recipient of memorial gifts, it's only appropriate that your presence is obvious. You might even want to provide flowers or a plant.

3. **Follow up within days.** Depending on the circumstances and the wishes of family members, set an appointment to meet and review memorial possibilities. Have a standard presentation developed — such as the example below — to outline gift possibilities.

Develop a presentation such as this to share with family members of the deceased.

Prepare Memorial Gift Options to Share

If memorial gifts amount to less than $1,000
Have a prepared wish list of needs — perhaps identified by your development committee — with attached dollar amounts. Include a range of dollar amounts and uses. This allows families to decide on the exact use of memorial funds without simply having funds disappear into your organization's annual budget.

Explain that the memorial — plus the names of all who contributed — will be listed in your organization's annual report of contributors.

For memorial gifts between $1,000 and $10,000
Once again, share a wish list of needs, only this time identify more significant needs that include naming opportunities based on the overall amount contributed toward the memorial. Memorial gifts totaling $2,000, for instance, could be used to name an item — a flowing water fountain or a meeting room table — while a gift of $9,000 might name an office or a particular room in honor of someone.

For memorial gifts that may amount to $10,000 or more
Gifts totaling $10,000 or more — even if given by family members over a period of years (or through a bequest) — could be used to establish various types of named endowment funds or to name even more significant physical projects (e.g., The Ben Michner Cancer Center, The Mark Steffenson Reading Room). Once again, it's helpful to have an identified list of needs. With this level of giving, however, it's important that the donor have some say in shaping the exact use of the gift so he/she develops a greater sense of ownership.

CREATING MEMORIAL, IN TRIBUTE GIFTS

Walkway Program Generates $41,000

Want to provide a great way for your constituents to remember loved ones and pay tribute to friends, family and associates — and raise money in the process? Follow The Morton Arboretum's (Lisle, IL) example by getting a tribute brick program underway.

The program was introduced in 2004 and so far has raised $41,000. The bricks are placed on The Tribute Walkway in the forecourt of the Arboretum's Visitor Center. The walkway currently has 54 bricks in place.

There are two sizes for the dedication bricks: 4 X 8 inch for a $500 donation; and 8 X 8 inch for a $1,000 donation. The Arboretum laser engraves the desired inscription; however, it is limited to an individual or family name, using up to two lines with 14 characters per line for the 4 X 8 inch bricks and up to four lines with 14 characters per line for the 8 X 8 inch bricks. They install the bricks twice a year.

"Donors are pleased with the program and are thrilled when their engraved brick is added to the walkway," says Kelli Bender, development coordinator. "Whether celebrating a birthday, anniversary or commemorating the life of a loved one, the tribute brick program serves as a source of meaningful recognition for many."

The tribute brick program is marketed through two printed brochures, which explain the program to potential tribute donors, the Arboretum's website, direct mail solicitation and electronic media.

Source: Kelli Bender, Development Coordinator, Donor Relations, The Morton Arboretum, Lisle, IL. Phone (630) 719-7976. E-mail: kbender@mortonarb.org

A great way to raise funds for a project is to offer donors affordable ways to honor loved ones.

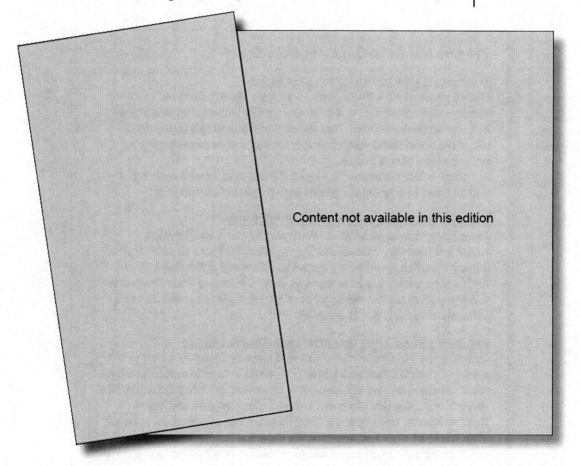

Content not available in this edition

CREATING MEMORIAL, IN TRIBUTE GIFTS

Giving Opportunities Start at $5,000 to Engage Donors

To involve people in the hospital's Imagine Campaign, officials with El Camino Hospital Foundation (Mountain View, CA) offer honor and memorial opportunities starting at $5,000.

Donors who wish to leave their philanthropic mark can give $5,000 for the organization's Nights at the Clinic program, $250,000 to name the laboratory, $1 million for an operating room, $3 million for the Oak Pavilion or up to $10 million to name the new main building.

To promote the opportunities, Lindsay Greensweig, director of major giving, says the foundation created folders to give to donors at one-on-one meetings, mail to prospective donors and distribute at VIP tours of the new hospital campus.

The folders include a campaign brochure that makes a compelling case for philanthropy with highlights of the new hospital campus; the quarterly campaign newsletter; brochures for hospital programs supported by the foundation; and the list of the honor and memorial opportunities.

To date, donors have made 10 honor and memorial gifts totaling $5 million.

The two-phase campaign is all-inclusive, focusing on the hospital program and bricks and mortar. The first phase, finished a year early, brought in $25 million in four years and focused on gaining philanthropic support for new programs.

The second phase, launched in September 2008, aims to raise another $25 million in three to five years to coincide with the hospital's golden anniversary. This campaign will focus more on the honor and memorial opportunities, while raising money for hospital programs.

The campaign is scheduled to conclude in 2013.

Source: Lindsay Greensweig, Director of Major Giving, El Camino Hospital Foundation, Mountain View, CA. Phone (650) 988-7849. E-mail: Lindsay_Greensweig@ elcaminohospital.org

Campaign Cabinet Acts As Community Liaison

Lindsay Greensweig, director of major giving, El Camino Hospital Foundation (Mountain View, CA), says its 15-member Imagine Campaign Cabinet serves as the foundation's liaison to the community, working to build relationships with current and prospective donors.

Once prospective donors are identified, cabinet members begin to build relationships, inviting them to large and small events (e.g., gala, golf tourney, VIP tours of new hospital campus, leadership briefings) and cultivate prospects one on one to learn their particular interests and concerns.

"These conversations provide us the opportunity to tell them about El Camino Hospital's achievements and aspirations," says Greensweig. "As we build these relationships and get to know our donors, we are able to determine their capacity and how best to approach them for a gift, including opportunities for honor and memorial."

Content not available in this edition

Provide would-be donors with a menu of naming gift opportunities that include price tags.

CREATING MEMORIAL, IN TRIBUTE GIFTS

Hospital Invites Donors to Sponsor Rooms

Mercy Medical Center Foundation (Cedar Rapids, IA) is inviting donors to sponsor a patient room or other areas on one of Mercy Medical Center's floors as part of its plan to convert all its hospital rooms to private single patient rooms. Donors can also sponsor the purchase of artwork.

In recognition of the person's sponsorship, an engraved plaque is affixed on the wall outside each room or suite, or beside the sponsored artwork. The plaque contains the name of the donors or the name of the persons they wish to memorialize with their gift. Donors are also listed in the foundation's annual report.

Since the campaign began in 2003, more than 100 of the hospital's 230 rooms have been sponsored, and they have raised a total of $500,000.

"Our room sponsorship campaign is a wonderful way for family and friends of patients to honor or memorialize a loved one or friend," says Sue Hawn, president. "It's also an opportunity for a donor to honor a physician or a member of the Mercy staff."

"With the focus of this project, we have the opportunity to reach out to donors who like to make gifts in honor or memory of loved ones, nurses or physicians," says Hawn. "It is a very visible project and offers a tangible way to give."

The campaign has been promoted primarily through direct mail, she says. A new direct mail piece was mailed at the end of July. Each direct mail piece includes a reply card and envelope. The cover letter is signed by Hawn and the chair of the foundation board.

"We also personalize some of the letters in the mailing, adding a note when we know that this opportunity to give might be of particular interest to the donor," she says. "The notes might say, 'Here's the information we talked about. I hope you'll find it to be an interesting opportunity.' Or, if one of their family members passed away, we would write a note saying that we thought they might be interested in sponsoring a room to memorialize 'X.'"

Hawn says they also have a general giving brochure that includes information about the room sponsorship campaign.

The cost to sponsor one patient room is $5,000. A suite sponsorship is $10,000. Other sponsorship opportunities include $1,000 for original corridor art, and $2,000 for crucifixes for the entire floor. Donors can also sponsor a nurses' station or a family waiting area for $10,000. An entire floor sponsorship is $1 million.

"With the focus of this project, we have the opportunity to reach out to donors who like to make gifts in honor or memory of loved ones, nurses or physicians," she says. "It is a very visible project and offers a tangible way to give. Many of our room sponsors come in to see their rooms."

Source: Sue Hawn, President, Mercy Medical Center Foundation, Cedar Rapids, IA. Phone (319) 398-6278. E-mail: shawn@mercycare.org

Pending Option Gives Grieving Donors Time

When a loved one dies, families can become overwhelmed with all of the arrangements, decisions and grief.

"Very often, when a family has lost a loved one, they are not ready to decide the details of how to memorialize them," says Bonny Kellermann, director of memorial gifts at MIT (Cambridge, MA). "Allowing a cushion of time to make this decision is greatly appreciated by the families."

MIT allows families to establish funds with a purpose to be determined later through their pending memorial gift accounts. The decision of what to use the funds for can be deferred for up to two years. When the account is established, families are informed that any funds not designated within two years will be used for unrestricted purposes.

The pending option gives families time to think about an appropriate, meaningful memorial and allows time for them to receive memorial gifts from other people, which can be a factor in determining how the fund will be used.

"Since the donors have the time to consider what is really important to them," Kellerman says, "they may be inclined to give more than they might have otherwise given."

Source: Bonny Kellermann, Director of Memorial Gifts, MIT, Cambridge, MA. Phone (617) 253-9722. E-mail: bonnyk@MIT.EDU

CREATING MEMORIAL, IN TRIBUTE GIFTS

Offer Options for Whom to Name

Truman State University (Kirksville, MO) suggests ideas for whom donors could name besides themselves. They suggest paying tribute or memorial to parents, grandparents, children or spouses; other family members; mentors; an organization; a place; a business or a business associate — through a naming gift.

They have also given some examples of how a tribute or memorial naming could be worded:

- "Virginia Young Stanton Garden"
- "Dr. John D. Black Memorial Scholarship"
- "Stanley & Doris Bohon Family Scholarship"
- "79th Field Hospital Scholarship"
- "Beta Tau Delta/Mary Evelyn Thurman Chemistry Laboratory"

The University has established 110 new funds in three years during their $30 million Bright Minds Bright Futures campaign, 70 of which were named.

Twenty of those named funds are memorials or tributes to others. Graduates have honored their professions through the creation of lectureships and speaker series, their parents through endowments for scholarships, student abroad stipends and research fellowships; or honored coaches or professors by naming buildings or scholarships for them.

"Tributes and memorials provide an opportunity to keep major gift conversations moving forward, particularly with individuals who are not interested in attaching their own names to a scholarship, program or facility," says Mark Gambaiana, vice president for university advancement.

Cultivation visits are the key starting point for determining who might be a candidate for making a tribute or memorial naming gift, he says: "In those visits, you need to determine if someone (a faculty member, staff, fellow student, or family member who may or may not have an association with your organization) has made a significant or life-changing impact on the prospect."

Some of the best questions Gambaiana says he has used to uncover that information include:

- What were some of your best experiences as a student here?
- In what positive ways has the university influenced your life?
- How did the university best prepare you for your career?

Source: Mark Gambaiana, Vice President for University Advancement, Truman State University, Kirksville, MO. Phone (660) 785-4133. E-mail: markg@truman.edu

When cultivating prospect donors, listen carefully for clues that may help determine options for memorial or in-tribute gifts

ESTABLISHING NAMED FUNDS THROUGH PLANNED GIFTS

People can establish named funds as outright gifts, they can establish them as planned gifts or they can do a combination of both. Planned gifts often times allow donors to make a more sizable gift that may otherwise be impossible to carry out. Here we will examine many ways in which a naming gift can be established or added to through planned gifts.

Approach Annual $1,000-plus Donors for Planned Gifts

How many annual contributors do you have at the $1,000-and-above level? What percentage of that group has made planned gift provisions for your organization?

Take steps to encourage and reassure those faithful and generous donors that their annual support will continue long after their lifetimes. Approach donors individually with invitations to make a planned gift that — after their lifetimes — will go to establish named endowment funds. Yearly interest from each fund will provide needed annual operations support (just as their annual contributions had done during their lifetimes).

Example: Assuming a donor had contributed $1,500 each year to your annual fund, it would take an endowment gift of $30,000 or more — based on an estimated 5 percent return — to yield what had been given yearly. In this instance, encourage the donor to consider a planned gift of not less than $30,000 to make certain his/her level of past support continues well into the future.

Planned gifts ensure a donor's contributions will continue long after their lifetimes.

Work to Identify and Cultivate Children of Wealth

It's common for most nonprofits to focus on those with existing wealth. To lay the groundwork for major gifts that may not materialize for 10 or 20 years, develop a plan aimed at cultivating children of wealth.

Your community is full of individuals in their 30s, 40s and even 50s who are not yet in positions enabling them to make five- or six-figure gifts but will be in 10 or 20 years by virtue of their positions or inherited wealth.

Begin to cultivate those up-and-comers now with a plan that's unique to your organization. Here's one generic scenario that helps illustrate how to do it:

1. Launch some sort of young leaders society that is exclusive to 30- to 50-year-olds who contribute $1,000 or more annually to your organization.

2. Create a steering committee made of those donors who can take ownership in the effort and design a plan catering to this age group's interests. The steering committee can come up with social activities, member perks, donor recognition ideas, etc.

3. Encourage the committee to establish an annual awards program that recognizes its members in various categories (e.g., professional achievement, philanthropic efforts, volunteer contributions, etc.).

When members turn 51, induct them into a more traditional, inclusive $1,000-and-above gift club. Hold an annual graduation ceremony that welcomes them into the older crowd.

Young Can Establish Planned Gifts, Too

Who says younger persons aren't interested in making planned gifts?

Even if younger constituency members do not receive every planned gift communication produced by your organization, it may be wise to market specific planned gift opportunities to them as well.

Consider the following possibilities:

- **Gift annuities honoring parents.** Why not encourage younger individuals to honor their parents or other older relatives with a named fund? Because the annuity is tied to the age of the older adults, the annual rate of return will be higher and more attractive to donors.

- **Life insurance policies.** Life insurance is often referred to as the affordable major gift since a major gift can be established using much small gifts equal to annual insurance premiums. (And premiums are lower at a younger age.)

- **Bequests.** Encourage younger donors to include bequests in their estate plans, regardless of amount.

ESTABLISHING NAMED FUNDS THROUGH PLANNED GIFTS

Help Planned Gift Prospects Visualize Their Capabilities

It's been demonstrated time and again that most planned gifts are given based on personal gratification of some form. Certainly tax consequences play a role in the gift giving process, but are generally secondary to fulfilling one or more personal needs.

So if most planned gifts are driven by some form of personal gratification — to help others and society, to leave a lasting legacy, to honor or memorialize someone — a donor's ability to visualize what his/her gift will accomplish is key to its realization.

Your ability to illustrate the before and after of a planned gift will play a critical role in convincing the would-be donor to commit. Your preparation in painting a picture of what a planned gift will accomplish for your institution and those you serve will help the prospect begin to experience the personal need — helping others, making a difference, ego gratification — that will make the individual want to make a bequest or some other form of a planned gift.

That's why it's so important to visualize what could be as you meet with and cultivate planned gift prospects. It's not enough to know the technical aspects and tax consequences of various planned gifts.

Utilize these techniques to help the prospect visualize how his/her planned gift could make a noticeable difference:

- Provide personal tours of your facilities, pointing out present services and comparing them to what could be offered with the realization of a major gift.

- As you meet with prospects, share and leave with them printed illustrations of named gift opportunities. One illustration may, for instance, describe what a $50,000 gift could accomplish in providing annual scholarships for needy students. Another may help to visualize how an endowed landscaping and maintenance fund will enhance your organization's environment and maintain it for years to come.

- Share specific examples of what past donors' bequests are accomplishing for your organization. In fact, share examples of what other donors' planned gifts have accomplished for other institutions. This is simply another way of visualizing what could happen if sufficient funds were made available.

In addition to helping donors see just what their gifts will accomplish, it's important to help them visualize the mechanics of how their gift is spent or invested (as in the case of an endowed gift). The more they understand, the more comfortable they will become in turning visions into reality.

Cosgrove University
Preparing Tomorrow's Leaders Today

NAMING GIFT CONSIDERATION

THE MARGARET AND TAYLOR ELLINGSON ENDOWED SCHOLARSHIP

Suggested Gift Amount: $100,000

Intent of Bequest
To assist junior and senior women attending Cosgrove University who intend to pursue health-related careers. Eligible students must have maintained a 3.4 grade point average or higher during their freshman and sophmore years. Financial need should also be taken into consideration.

How the Funds Will Be Invested
Once this $100,000 bequest is realized, it will be invested as a part of Cosgrove University's endowment portfolio. (See attached endowment report.) Annual interest from the fund will be awarded to deserving students who meet the guidelines set forth by Margaret and Taylor Ellingson. In recent years, the university's board of directors has approved an annual payout of 7 percent to ensure the preservation of the gift's principal for generations to come.

Therefore, if the annual interest rate remains constant, $7,000 will be available each year for scholarship awards.

Procedure for Annual Awards
At the request of Margaret and Taylor Ellingson, annual awards will be made through the Office of Financial Aid in cooperation with faculty representatives from the science/health-related disciplines.

Preparing Future Generations of Caring Health Professionals
Consider, for example, seven deserving Cosgrove University students each receiving a $1,000 award in any given year. Using that example, a gift such as this could in one decade assist as many as 70 students to receive a degree they might not otherwise have been able to do.

Over a 10-year period, as many as 70 graduates could be moving on to seek additional education or entering health-related careers. What a marvelous way to help so many young people! What a marvelous investment in our society's future!

ESTABLISHING NAMED FUNDS THROUGH PLANNED GIFTS

Approach Named Endowment Donors for Planned Gifts

Here's a way to encourage endowment donors to consider a planned gift.

If your organization already has a good number of named endowment gifts in place, use a variety of methods that encourage those endowment donors to add to their funds with planned gifts. These donors make great planned gift prospects since they have already demonstrated their ability to make sizeable outright gifts to your organization. Plus, the addition of planned gifts will one day help to ensure that their endowments live up to their intended use far into the future.

Here are some ways to market planned gifts to endowment gift donors:

1. Get to know and meet regularly with all endowment gift donors.

2. Do an article about an endowment gift donor who added to his/her endowment with a planned gift.

3. Host an estate planning seminar geared specifically to endowment donors. Earmark a portion of the event to focus on issues related to your organization's endowment (e.g., policies, performance, investment philosophy, etc.).

4. When publishing lists of endowment donors, highlight those who will be adding to their funds with planned gifts.

5. When preparing annual updates for those who have established endowment funds, include "what if" examples relating to possible planned gifts.

Naming a Space Using Planned Gift, Good or Bad?

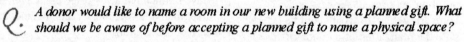

Q. *A donor would like to name a room in our new building using a planned gift. What should we be aware of before accepting a planned gift to name a physical space?*

Be cautious when using a planned gift to name a physical space.

Former planned giving director Kurt Moore, now director of corporate research and development for Florida State University (Tallahassee), cautions against naming a building, facility or even a professorship with anything but an irrevocable gift.

That means no bequests, testamentary trusts, designations as beneficiary of insurance, retirement plans, or commercial annuities, "nor anything that can be changed or revoked by the prospect," Moore says. "Also, exclude irrevocable deferred gifts where the donor reserves the right to change the recipient of the trust remainder to another eligible 501(c)(3) recipient."

More acceptable forms of named planned gifts, says Moore, include:

• Irrevocable deferred gifts of charitable remainder trusts

• Charitable gift annuities

• Pooled income funds

• Life estates or other legally binding arrangement.

Also, immediate gifts of paid-up life insurance policies or irrevocable lead trusts can qualify, he says.

"Proceeds of a charitable gift annuity may be able to be used immediately, depending on your state's regulations and your institution's policy regarding management of your reserve fund," says Moore. "It is to the institution's benefit to have a written policy on using planned gifts in naming opportunities."

Source: Kurt R. Moore, CFRE, Director of Corporate Research & Development, Florida State University, Tallahassee, FL. Phone (850) 645-5753. E-mail: kmoore@mailer.fsu.edu

NAMING GIFT OPPORTUNITIES: How to Successfully Secure More Naming Gifts

TYING NAMING GIFTS INTO CAPITAL CAMPAIGNS

Naming gifts tend to fit very appropriately into capital campaigns since the aim of such campaigns is toward major gifts or $25,000 or more. The campaign presents a tidy menu of gift opportunities — both capital and endowment — that can be named depending on the gift amount.

Naming Opportunities Introduce Potential Donors to Campaign

Naming opportunities add personality and approachability to a major campaign.

Offering donors the opportunity to assign their names to specific areas of support is proving invaluable to organizers of the $88 million Open the Door to Hope capital campaign for Camillus House (Miami, FL), says Gloria Barbier, vice president of institutional advancement. Naming opportunities are described on the campaign website (www.camillus-odh.org/naming_opportunities/) with cost and what the cost supports.

"These descriptions serve as the first introduction to our naming opportunities," Barbier says. "By providing more detailed information about our buildings to be named, we give donors an opportunity to read about them before we meet with them in person."

To date, donors have signed on to support several buildings, including the Intake Center ($500,000), Career Center ($5 million) and Dining & Nutrition Center ($3.5 million).

When a naming opportunity is taken, staff adds a flashing light icon next to its name on the website, Barbier says. "For example, the Administration Building has been named by the Knight Foundation. When you click on the flashing light by the Administration Building under Naming Opportunities, it says 'This building has been named after the Knight Foundation,' and describes the amount given ($3 million) and a link to the press release announcing the gift."

Indicating that a naming opportunity is taken allows other prospective donors to see how Camillus House promotes its named spaces, says Barbier. Doing so has also created competition among potential funders, she says. "For example, if there are three large banks in town and two have already named a building, the third is going to want to participate too. It creates a sense of urgency to be part of what we're doing."

Most naming opportunities currently on Camillus House's campaign website are reserved for foundations, corporations or individuals with a high capacity to give and a close relationship to Camillus House, says Barbier. To provide the opportunity for others to support the campaign, plans are to add naming opportunities for lower-level gifts (e.g., $10,000 to $50,000) and launch a brick campaign for gifts at the $250 to $1,000 level.

Camillus House representatives meet one on one with donor prospects, presenting them with a package of materials that includes a list of major naming opportunities and costs. The package also includes a more detailed list of all of their naming opportunities, including descriptions on number of spaces available, square footage of each area, a short description of the area to be named and cost to do so.

Source: Gloria Barbier, Vice President of Institutional Advancement, Camillus House, Miami, FL.
Phone (305) 226-4558. E-mail: barbierg@camillus.org

Valuing Naming Opportunities

Gloria Barbier, vice president of institutional advancement, Camillus House (Miami, FL), describes how her organization determined value of naming opportunities in its Open the Door to Hope capital campaign:

"We took into account the price per square foot of the space being named and the value of the program related to the services it provides. We calculated the square footage of the entire facility and then went building by building to calculate the square footage of each building. To calculate the value of the program, we looked at the program's success rate.

"For example, the success rate for those individuals engaged in active treatment through Camillus House's Institute of Social & Personal Adjustment is nearly 90 percent, making it one of the most successful, either publicly or privately funded programs in the country. Cost to name this building is $7 million. Even if this wasn't the largest building, the value of the program is priceless, and so the naming opportunity is the largest in our campaign."

TYING NAMING GIFTS INTO CAPITAL CAMPAIGNS

Nothing's Too Small to Offer as a Naming Opportunity

Light switches, phones, thermostats and exterior lighting are just some of the objects donors can choose to fund in a $22 million campaign for Detroit Public Television (Detroit, MI). A portion of the money will go to build the Riley Broadcast Center.

Naming opportunities begin at $56.

"We're going to name everything," says Trisha Cohn, donor relations coordinator. "It has been a great way to get people involved in the campaign. We're providing naming opportunities that give everyone who appreciates Detroit Public Television recognition in areas to suit their interests, whether it's education, local productions, the arts or the environment."

A five-day on-air campaign launched the effort's general membership phase and highlighted naming opportunities.

Many nonprofits can gain success in a campaign by offering less expensive items for naming.

"Many gave at the $56 level," Cohn says. "The most popular item to name was a telephone. We received many pledges from new donors," she says of the effort that raised $100,000.

The station's naming opportunities are also offered on its website, where visitors can search for adoptable items by keyword or donation amount, or by browsing the full list of items.

Donors of $1,000 or more can pay in installments of up to 36 months. Donors of $56 to $999 can pay in installments of up to 12 months.

"We of course couldn't put names on each individual item, so we decided to recognize our named donors with plaques," says Cohn. "Different plaques will recognize different items or areas of the building. For example, we will have a separate plaque for studio items.

"We chose to display the plaques in our lobby because we wanted them to be where people could see them as they come into the building."

All namings are in perpetuity.

A virtual tour offered on the station's website also allows donors and prospective donors to view named items (www.dptv.org/support/capcampaign.shtml).

Source: Trisha Cohn, Donor Relations Coordinator, Detroit Public TV, Wixom, MI. Phone (248) 305-3739. E-mail: tcohn@dptv.org

Study Named Endowments to Forecast Campaign Gifts

If you're planning a capital campaign that includes an endowment component, be sure to review all existing named endowment funds as one component of your overall goal-setting procedures.

Trying to get an idea of where your campaign gifts will come from and how much you might expect from each source? Analyze your exsisting named endowments to estimate gift potential from these sources.

Because existing endowment donors will be among your best prospects for future endowment gifts, it makes sense to estimate potential endowment gifts from those sources. Many of those current donors will look favorably at adding to their existing endowments, while simultaneously participating in your campaign.

Estimate what each donor might be willing to add to his/her existing endowment fund as part of a campaign pledge to be paid out over a one- to five-year period. Also, if your campaign will include irrevocable planned gifts, some donors may choose to make a planned gift as well (or in lieu of an outright gift).

TYING NAMING GIFTS INTO CAPITAL CAMPAIGNS

Study Big Picture to Set Naming Opportunities

Allowing naming opportunities is helping organizers of a $25-million capital campaign for St. John Health Foundation (Madison Heights, MI) raise the funds needed to build an inpatient hospital at a new Providence Park campus (Novi, MI).

Debbie Condino, interim foundation president, says the 200-acre health park site of the new hospital offers several unique naming opportunities, such as a health trail, atrium elevators, green space, pond, connector tunnel and the hospital itself.

"The naming rights to the new hospital will be the most prominent, particularly since this will be the first completely new hospital built from scratch in southeast Michigan in more than 20 years," she says. "The hospital will have all private patient rooms, another unique feature that has provided us with an additional 200 individual naming opportunities for the campaign."

Given the unique scope and size of the project, says Condino, they carefully reviewed the plans for the hospital to determine not only the spaces that would have the most appeal to potential donors as naming opportunities, but the services that would be among the new hospital's specialties and strengths, such as neurosciences and women's health, that could provide naming opportunities as well.

Naming costs range from $15 million to name the hospital to $2,500 to dedicate a tree on the campus. So far, donors have purchased 65 naming opportunities.

To determine naming opportunity costs, Condino says they used this criteria:

- Size, scope and visibility of the specific area.

- Naming opportunities from other capital campaigns, including those associated with St. John Health and Ascension Health.

- Initial prospect research, which indicated the interests and capabilities of their campaign prospect base.

"We also considered market benchmarks and what other like projects and facilities both outside and inside health care command in terms of levels for naming," she says.

Source: Debbie Condino, Interim President, St. John Health Foundation, Madison Heights, MI. Phone (586) 582-7500. E-mail: debbie.condino@ stjohn.org

This brochure is helping officials with St. John Health Foundation (Madison Heights, MI) detail naming opportunities as part of a $25-million capital campaign to build a new hospital.

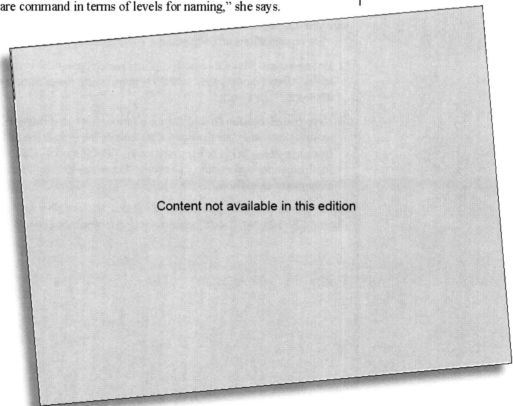

Content not available in this edition

TYING NAMING GIFTS INTO CAPITAL CAMPAIGNS

Hospital Offers Floors of Naming Opportunities

To solicit support for a $208 million capital campaign, development staff at Kosair Children's Hospital and Children's Hospital Foundation (Louisville, KY) offers naming opportunities for its facilities, programs, professorships and fellowships.

Donors can name a variety of rooms on the hospital's nine floors, including the emergency/trauma center for $5 million, one of 20 treatment rooms for $25,000 or a child psychiatric annex for $250,000.

Donors have already paid to name the hospital's radiology department and MRI suite. Donors can also choose to name several programs for gifts of $50,000 to $500,000 or endow several clinical chairs and fellowships for $1 million each. Professorships and fellowships are available for naming with gifts of $270,000 to $500,000, depending on the program and position.

Several months into the campaign, the foundation had named some 30 rooms, positions or projects, raising a combined $10 million.

"While some donors are interested in naming, others are motivated by different components of the program," says Lynnie Meyer, the foundation's chief development officer. "Naming opportunities can be used as a discussion point for those who do have an interest in naming."

Before determining naming gift thresholds, carefully research the market and the cost of each project.

Before setting gift levels, Meyer says, the foundation staff and hospital leadership carefully researched the market and the cost of each project as well as their campaign feasibility study and donor base.

They set naming gift levels at roughly 50 percent of the total cost of each project, based on a rule of thumb they had learned in their research, says Meyer: "It was only used as a guide, however, and adjusted downward based on other information. For example, half of a $20 million project may be $10 million, but if we didn't have that many $10 million donor prospects, we lowered the naming level to $7 million or $8 million so that it would make sense for us."

Once foundation staff and hospital leadership agreed on the ranges, they presented them to the CEO and president, who signed off on them, she says, noting: "It's important to make sure you have institutional support."

For organizations offering naming opportunities, Meyer advises:

❑ **Be consistent.** Make sure project prices match across the system. Set up credible gift tables. "Don't be desperate and allow someone to name something for far less than what it's worth," she says.

❑ **Keep the discussion tied to the case for support and mission.** Don't let naming opportunities dominate your dialogue. Concentrate the discussion on how someone can transform something in his or her community. "The majority of people are not making the gift for the naming opportunity," she says, "but rather the impact the program will have on the community as a whole."

Source: Lynnie Meyer, Chief Development Officer, Children's Hospital Foundation, Louisville, KY. Phone (502) 629-8060. E-mail: lynnie.meyer@nortonhealthcare.org

TYING NAMING GIFTS INTO CAPITAL CAMPAIGNS

Offer Naming Opportunities to Employee Divisions

Jawonio, an affiliate of the Cerebral Palsy Associations of New York, offered its employee divisions the opportunity to name an area within its newly renovated building at the conclusion of the organization's capital campaign in exchange for conducting their own internal campaigns. Four divisions agreed to do so, coming up with goals ranging from $5,000 to $15,000.

Two years into the three-year campaign, one division has so far exceeded its $10,000 goal by more than $1,500, and its members figure they will raise $15,000 by the end of the campaign.

The total goal was $50,000, but Jawanio officials expect to exceed that goal by $10,000.

Each division chose a capital campaign dedication that related to the services they offer. They also came up with their own goal and method of raising funds. One division partnered with a local nursery for a plant sale; others held bake sales, car washes, raffles, etc. Most chose to make their gift via voluntary payroll deduction of $1 to $5 per pay period, with their division receiving credit toward their pledge. Employees giving $100 or more received a brick on Jawonio's Walk of Achievement.

"We wanted to provide a way for employees to make a gift to our capital campaign that would allow them to buy into it at a minimum level while at the same time raising major funds," says Jeff Kassover, CFRE, director of development.

In introducing this plan to Jawonio's employees, Kassover wanted to make sure everyone felt they were consulted about it. He sent a questionnaire to all employees explaining the plan, and asking how they felt about it. About 125 of the organization's 700 employees responded; 80 percent of those were in favor of the plan. To kick off the internal campaign, the organization's eight senior staff members each made gifts totaling $20,000.

Source: Jeff Kassover, CFRE, Director of Development, Jawonio, New City, NY. Phone (845) 634-4648 ext. 1342. E-mail: jeff.kassover@jawonio.org

Give your employees a voice in naming opportunities. Doing so may motivate them to give more enthusiastically.

Naming Gift Opportunities: How to Successfully Secure More Naming Gifts.
Edited by Scott C. Stevenson.
© 2009 Stevenson, Inc. Published 2009 by Stevenson, Inc.

STEWARDING AND RECOGNIZING NAMED DONORS

Anyone who has the capability and prodivity to make a major naming gift obviously deserves recognition unless they prefer anonymity. Nevertheless, anyone making gifts of that magnitude deserve proper stewardship. It's in their best interest, and yours, to share the impact their gifts are having on your organization and those you serve.

Program Encourages Repeat Gifts to Named Funds

Only a few months after The Christian Broadcasting Network launched its Living Tributes program, the frequency and size of Living Tribute/Memorial gifts increased three-fold, says Kevin Feldman, director of grant development and manager of special fundraising projects.

Tribute Web pages allow donors to visualize their gift and also allow those who are being honored to visualize it as well.

Living tribute/memorials allow donors to make a tribute gift to, for example, their children, and then make annual gifts to CBN in their children's names because the organization has established a fund in their names. The donor can also invite other friends and relatives to make additional contributions to the fund. "The fund doesn't have to be restricted, unless the donor has asked to designate the money for a particular program," says Feldman.

As an incentive to continue making gifts to the fund, CBN creates, with the donor's permission, a Web page to honor the persons the fund was set up to honor. The Web pages are accessible through CBN's website (www.cbn.com/giving/livingtributes/). Each Web page has a statement such as, "You can make a Tribute Gift to The Christian Broadcasting Network in honor of the Jones kids by clicking on the link below." The hyperlink takes donors directly to their website's giving pages where people can make an online gift using a credit card. Motivation codes in the hyperlink help the organization track what living tribute generated the gift.

"While we have had many requests for Web page tributes, we were surprised at the number of donors who didn't want the Web pages created for them," Feldman says. "The fact that we had something unique to market that offered more value to donors motivated more people to make tribute gifts regardless of whether they wanted the Web page."

Here's one person's reaction to the program: "This is going to be big in the future, I'm sure. It's a wonderful way to honor and give at the same time — a great gift idea."

Source: Kevin D. Feldman, Director of Grant Development, and Manager of Special Fundraising Projects, The Christian Broadcasting Network, Virginia Beach, VA. Phone (757) 226-3574.

Urge Named Endowment Donors to Add to Funds

Officials with the Minnesota Historical Society proactively encourage named endowment fund donors to add to their funds — with impressive results.

The society's named endowment funds have increased from 23 to 66, and the society has gone from no pooled named endowment funds to nine. The organization's deferred gift portfolio grew from 22 to 113 provisions, 48 of which have a combined estimated value of $8.5 million. Also, the society's identified prospects grew in number from 30 to 876.

"Considering that a full-fledged named endowment fund starts at $50,000, those numbers are pretty significant," says Keith Bartz, the society's former director of planned and major gifts.

Bartz outlines four major methods society officials use to encourage this:

1. Having donors start the fund with a cash gift and supplement it with a deferred gift (typically a will provision), which allows donors to see the fund's benefits in their lifetime.

2. Sending donors annual endowed fund reports to build confidence and affinity for the fund. Reports include cover letters detailing fund performance and stating what program areas benefited from the fund in the last year. The program person will also typically write a letter to represent the fund's recipients.

3. Asking for an additional gift after appropriate cultivation.

4. Showing donors the valuable work and additional need of the program area or historic site the fund benefits, typically with visits or staff contact.

Source: Keith W. Bartz, Former Director of Planned Gifts/Major Gifts, Minnesota Historical Society, St. Paul, MN. Phone (651) 205-4575. E-mail: keith.bartz@mnhs.org

STEWARDING AND RECOGNIZING NAMED DONORS

Inventory What's Named On Your Grounds

Have you ever inventoried every physical structure — buildings, offices, auditoriums, roadways, etc. — named for someone throughout your campus or facility?

After developing your list, determine which of these named structures does not have an accompanying endowment fund intended to cover its future maintenance and enhancement costs. Those that aren't endowed provide the perfect opportunity to go back to the family, friends or business associates of the named individual to seek restricted endowment support. It doesn't really matter if the named individual is no longer living. Approach the individual's heirs. Or, if the structure is named for a business or foundation, approach those presently in charge.

There's a certain pride of ownership associated with having named structures. Those who made the initial naming gift, and often those associated with the donor, like to know their building, office or whatever is being fully maintained and updated. An endowment fund earmarked for that named structure ensures funds will always be available for ongoing maintenance.

Having a list of all named structures provides you with a good tool for procuring future named endowments from past donors.

Select the Proper Wording for Plaques

Cheryl L. Kester, director of grants and foundation relations for John Brown University (Siloam Springs, AR), did extensive research when preparing her recommendations for the naming plaques to be placed in the university's most recently constructed building. She shares her process for selecting the proper wording for their naming plaques:

"I examined the plaques already on campus and consulted colleagues at other campuses to see what they do. In our case, we wished to maintain some similarity and tradition, so I tried to follow precedents set by earlier campus plaques as much as possible. I am now developing standards so the next round of plaques will be simple.

"I drew up suggested wording for each plaque, and then contacted the donor for permission to place the plaque and approval of wording. In all cases, whether the naming was for a foundation or individual, we followed the wishes of the donor. I believe the university would only get involved if the donor suggested something that was potentially offensive. Fortunately, that situation has not arisen on our campus."

Source: Cheryl L. Kester, Director of Grants and Foundations, John Brown University, Siloam Springs, AR. Phone (479) 524-7447. E-mail: cherylk@jbu.edu

Here are examples of the plaques displayed at John Brown University. Names have been changed to protect the privacy of the donors.

The B. R. Brown Engineering Building
Presented by Mr. & Mrs. B. R. Brown
1962
~
In recognition of a major gift by
Mr. and Mrs. John Doe
Mrs. Janet Doe
~
John A. Jones Gallery Concourse
This facility provided through the generosity of the
Arkansas Endowment, Inc.
~
This lobby furnished through the generosity of
Mr. and Mrs. Janet Doe in honor of the music of
Mr. Paul Aurandt
~
The furnishings for this facility provided
through the generosity of
Mrs. Janet Doe
~
Doe Student Lounge Sponsor:
The John Doe Family
Miami, Florida
~
The Does General Biology Laboratory
In Honor of Dr. John A. Does
and his service to John Brown University
1960-1984
~
Equipment in this laboratory
provided by a generous gift from the
May B. Funds Trust
~
In grateful recognition of the
John and Janet Doe Foundation
Whose gracious gift made possible this sanctuary
balcony addition.
Dedicated to the glory of God
this 26th day of October 1990.

STEWARDING AND RECOGNIZING NAMED DONORS

Follow Up With Named Gift Donors

Here's an exercise with a dual purpose: Meet individually with everyone who has established a named gift. Explain that you want to improve future marketing efforts and sales skills. Ask those donors to identify what they have found to be most rewarding about the gifts they have made.

If you listen carefully, their responses will provide you with valuable ammunition you can use when approaching new prospects. Equally important, however, these donors will be articulating aloud what most energizes them about their past philanthropic actions, and that just might lead to their next big gift.

Keeping in touch with named gift donors helps set the stage for additional gifts.

Share Named Funds With Your Constituents

Looking for worthwhile content for your regularly published newsletter or magazine? Make a point to always include a brief article or photo and caption showcasing some of your named funds. Doing so allows you to plant seeds among your publication's readers while, at the same time, giving some deserved recognition to those who established those funds.

Ideas for such newsletter or magazine articles may include:

✓ A photo of scholarship recipients from a particular named scholarship along with mention of who established the fund, how long it's been in existence and the number of students that fund has benefited over time.

✓ A photo and brief article of a newly renovated space that is the result of a particular named maintenance fund.

✓ An interview with a lecturer whose presentation was made possible through a named lecture fund.

Celebrate the Activation of a Named Fund

When long-term pledges reach their final payment, do something to recognize not only the fund, but also the person who made the fund possible.

Seven years ago, a donor pledged $25,000 to establish a named endowment fund at your organization. The final payment is coming up, and the fund will soon kick in. How will you mark the occasion?

Donors often wait several years — until the fund reaches a certain level — before witnessing the fruits of their investments. Make a point to celebrate when a named endowment fund activates. Invite the donor to your premises to show what fund proceeds will accomplish. Provide a written summary of the fund's impact for the first year. Above all, recognize the culmination of their efforts when the day finally arrives!

STEWARDING AND RECOGNIZING NAMED DONORS

Approach the Children of Named Gift Donors

Are you adequately evaluating the potential of gifts from children of past and present donors — those who have already established named gifts? Whoever has given generous support in the past will possibly have children who also have substantial assets. In addition, constituents of modest means may have children whose career achievements have afforded them the ability to make a substantial gift to your cause.

While the children of your donors and noncontributing constituents may have established other philanthropic interests during their lifetimes, their parents establish an automatic link with your cause.

So how can you establish a plan for researching, identifying, cultivating and soliciting selected children of constituents? Here is one possible scenario:

1. **Develop a list of wealthy offspring prospects.** Whether it's staff driven or you establish a special committee, carefully scrutinize donor and constituent records to reveal any names of children who might have major gift potential.

2. **Add to your list of next-generation prospects.** Send an open invitation to your constituency — in a separate direct mail piece or as an article in your newsletter or magazine — inviting them to have their children's names included in your mailing list. Review all names that are shared with you to determine if they should be included among your wealthy offspring list.

3. **Begin making introductions.** Once you have a list of viable prospects in place, begin making face-to-face contact to introduce your cause, explain the linkage between your cause and the prospect's parents and begin a cultivation process. (These face-to-face visits will also screen and prioritize those with whom you come in contact.)

4. **Explore ways to "honor thy father and thy mother."** As cultivation continues, explore naming gift opportunities in which the offspring could establish a fund in tribute to or in memory of one or both parents. If the parent had already established a fund or made a naming gift to your institution in the past, determine the child's interest in adding to that fund or, in the case of a named capital gift such as a building or a room, creating a maintenance endowment that would cover future upkeep and renovation costs.

5. **Publicize your successes.** Whenever a constituent's child chooses to make a major contribution, seek permission to publicize the gift as much as possible as a way to plant seeds in the minds of other constituents' children. If you have enough children who step forward with generous gifts, you might choose to establish a separate committee, advisory group or prestigious society to promote this unique alliance with your organization (e.g., The Next Generation Society).

If you give sufficient attention to cultivating relationships with children of donors and other constituents, you will find ample gift potential within this group.

Develop a message that encourages major donors to add their childrens' names to your mailing list.

---

*FRIENDS OF
MAKE-A-WISH FOUNDATION*
Your Family Is Our Family —

We're grateful to have you as a faithful friend and contributor. In fact, we take great pride in considering you as a member of our extended family. Your caring and generosity have impacted many lives in very positive ways.

If you have grown children who might appreciate learning more about us and the work we do, we welcome having them on our mailing list. Simply complete the information below, return it to us and we'll send our most recent newsletter along with a personal note of welcome.

Since you have been so committed to our mission all these years, it only makes sense that we would extend an invitation to your children to continue your example of leadership.

Thank you in advance for making your family a part of our extended family.

Your Name_____ Phone_____

Please add the following names of our children to your mailing list:

Name(s)_____
Address_____
City_____ State____ ZIP _____

Name(s)_____
Address_____
City_____ State____ ZIP _____

Return to: Friends of Make-a-Wish Foundation, PO Box 3002, Harrison, CO 80309.

STEWARDING AND RECOGNIZING NAMED DONORS

Look to Your Donors for Naming Ideas

Sometimes, the appropriate name is an easy choice.

While looking into creating a consecutive giving society, staff with Occidental College (Los Angeles, CA) found that one donor couple — John and Addie McMenamin — had faithfully given to the college every year since graduating in 1940.

In honor of the McMenamins' generosity, Occidental staff decided to name the new consecutive giving society — which recognizes donors who give at least five consecutive years — the McMenamin Society.

"Remarkably, the McMenamins are not only alumni, but John is an emeritus biology professor," says Jim Tranquada, director of communications. "Addie is the former director of alumni relations, and their two sons are Oxy graduates. They have truly given to Oxy on almost every conceivable level, and we couldn't find a better pair to honor."

All donors of five or more consecutive years automatically become members of the McMenamin Society. Launched in fall 2007, the society has about 4,800 members.

"While major donors get the most attention, regular donors of smaller gifts are the backbone of the annual fund and our alumni participation rate," says Tranquada.

To introduce the new giving society, officials announced it in an annual publication called "Occidental Today," says Tranquada. "We are still strategizing additional ways to market the society and how to recognize members."

Source: Jim Tranquada, Director of Communications, Occidental College, Los Angeles, CA. Phone (323) 259-2990. E-mail: jtranqua@oxy.edu

Make donor recognition a top priority. Put some thought into your donor recognition clubs or societies, possibly by naming them after one of your most principal donors.

The annual publication of Occidental College (Los Angeles, CA), "Occidental Today," prominently features Class of 1940 alums John and Addie McMenamin as it introduces the consecutive giving society named in their honor.

Lightning Source UK Ltd.
Milton Keynes UK
UKOW01f0821020813

214783UK00006B/154/P